Origins of the Book:
From Papyrus to Codex

Mohamed A. Hussein

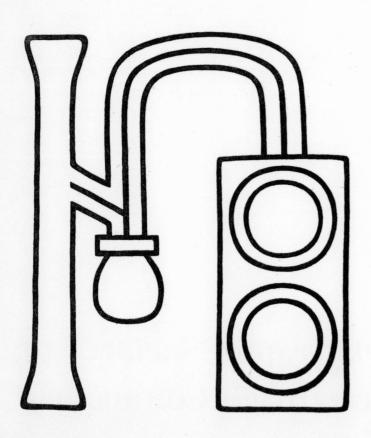

Origins of the Book

Egypt's
contribution to
the development
of the book
from papyrus
to codex

New York Graphic Society Ltd.
Greenwich, Connecticut

Advisors and Editors

Preface/Historical Survey: Wolfgang Müller
The Pharaonic Period: Renate Krauspe
The Greco-Roman Period: Wolfgang Müller
The Coptic Book: Wolfgang Müller
The Book in Islamic Egypt: Ulrich Luft

Translated by Dorothy Jaeschke and Douglas Sharp

Standard Book Number 8212-0446-7
Library of Congress Catalog Card Number 73-181343

First published in the United States of America in 1972
by New York Graphic Society Ltd., Greenwich, Connecticut.

Original edition © 1970 by Edition Leipzig

Printed in Germany by Druckerei Fortschritt Erfurt
Design by Volker Küster
Text illustrations by Inge Gohrisch

Contents

Preface

One of the many matter-of-fact things of our life is certainly the book which we see in various shapes, sizes, forms and layouts. It is probably only rarely that the reader poses a question about the origin and the development of the book as permanent carrier of literature from its beginnings to our time. Nevertheless, the question merits pondering and the answer shows that the early form of book, a roll, was quite different from the one we are familiar with: a codex consisting of several quires, of pages which can be turned over. The question leads us back to the history of antiquity, to the past and to remote places.

It was a long process during which the oldest forms of society developed and classes, states and autocratic structures with the economic superiority of a minority—the military, legal and religious power of a king—came into being. This development started very early—roughly at the beginning of the third millennium B.C.—in the south of Mesopotamia and in Egypt. States took different forms and to the extent to which man became aware of himself as someone acting or suffering at the commandment of the gods, he started to invent a script and to preserve names and events in writing. Although the first inscriptions were made on stones and clay, Egyptians found in their Nile delta the papyrus plant which— useful for many things—was to gain such importance as a writing material that it was only superseded by parchment, a leather tanned to extreme thinness, and paper, thousands of years later. It was thus Egypt which created the oldest form of book: a roll of papyrus sheets glued together. This form remained in use well into the era of Roman rule, until approximately the 4th century A.D., as the most important form for literature and documents. The codex, the book in quires and written on both sides of the page with which we are familiar, came into being towards the end of the Roman Republic with the advent of Christianity; it slowly became accepted in Egypt as well and later became the main book form in Europe, first on parchment and then on paper.

The purpose of this volume is to record and illustrate the most important phases of the evolution from the papyrus roll to the paper codex in Egypt, with its vitality and cultural continuity from the early era of the Pharaohs to the Arab Middle Ages in its various languages and scripts. This book cannot, of course, make claim to be a reference work on the history of literature, scripts or books; its aim is to provide the reader with an answer to the question about the origins of the book by presenting a small selection from an almost overwhelming mass of material.

For the American or European reader it may be particularly interesting to receive this answer from an Egyptian scholar whose assessment is made with full consciousness of the rich traditions of his homeland. Unfortunately his premature death prevented him from making a final revision of the text. Since the great archaeological excavations of the 19th and 20th centuries the scripts of ancient Egypt —both in roll and book form—have filled the museums and libraries of many countries in great number and are today among the gems of every manuscript collection.

For permission to use photographs and other material the publisher wishes to express his indebtedness to the following libraries, museums and collections:

Berlin, Deutsche Staatsbibliothek; Berlin, Staatliche Museen, Ägyptisches Museum, Papyrus-Sammlung; Dublin, Chester Beatty Library; Geneva, Bodmer Library; Cairo, Egyptian Museum; Cairo, Coptic Museum; Cairo, Museum of Islamic Art; Cairo, National Library; Leipzig, Karl Marx University, Ägyptisches Museum; London, British Museum; New York, Metropolitan Museum of Art; Paris, National Library; Washington, Freer Gallery of Art; Vienna, Kunsthistorisches Museum; Vienna, National Library.

The concluding bibliography is a brief summary of works of especial importance for the relevant sections and which contain valuable source material for anybody wishing to delve more deeply into the subject matter. It makes no claim to completeness.

Historical Survey

The civilisation of the ancient world had its cradle in the Near East, especially in Egypt and Mesopotamia, in Central Asia, on the coast of the Aegean Sea and on the Aegean Islands. From the Near East it then spread to the West. The first peak of ancient culture was already reached by Egypt and the civic states situated between the Euphrates and the Tigris in the 3rd millennium B.C.; a new flowering was experienced in Egypt and on Crete in the 2nd millennium and later by the Kingdoms of Assyria, Babylonia and Persia in the 8th, 7th and 6th centuries B.C.

The culture of the Ancient East lasted for nearly three thousand years, from the beginning of the 3rd millennium B.C. to the 1st century A.D., i.e. for a period nearly twice as long as that during which European culture developed.

The creative period of the Greeks lasted roughly from the 9th century B.C. to the 2nd century A.D. and Greek culture and civilisation only became predominant in the world as a result of fruitful contact with Eastern cultures after the conquest of the East by Alexander the Great.

There is a wealth of architectural and written evidence provided by pyramids, temples and tombs, statues, reliefs, paintings, stone inscriptions and thousands of papyri and ostraca (fragments of tablets) preserved by the dry soil of the country on the Nile. This makes it possible to trace and interpret Egyptian culture in all its epochs. In the 3rd century B.C., at the time of the Macedonian king Ptolemy II Philadelphus, the Egyptian priest Manetho wrote a history of Egypt. This work written in Greek, a large part of which has unfortunately not survived, stresses the unity of Upper and Lower Egypt as a single kingdom. From time immemorial the great River Nile provided easy means of access between various settlements and localities along its banks and facilitated uniformity of culture and language.

Neither the brief Assyrian conquest by Esarhaddon in 671 B.C. nor the longer period of Persian rule starting with the conquest of Egypt by Cambyses in 525 B.C. had a lasting influence on this ancient culture. It was only under the Macedonian rule of the Ptolemies, which lasted for 300 years, that Greek ideas and culture penetrated into the valley of the Nile in the wake of Hellenic and Hellenized mercenaries, merchants, artisans, artists and scholars. For centuries Alexandria was the intellectual centre of the ancient world. Greek became the official language and remained so even after the battle of Actium in 31 B.C. when Octavianus—better known as Augustus—made Egypt a part of the Roman Empire and for a long time the granary of Rome. The universal Hellenic outlook, however, was limited to the upper classes of the rich province. Temple buildings with their reliefs and inscriptions as well as the ritual of the dead remained Egyptian. And Isis, to whom worshippers erected shrines in many parts of the Roman Empire, was still an Egyptian goddess. But Coptic, the final stage of the Egyptian language, was decisively influenced by Christianity; in translating the Holy Scriptures the Coptic scribes adapted the Greek alphabet, thereby enabling reproduction of the entire phonetic range. With the Arab conquest in the middle of the 7th century A.D. the country on the Nile entered a new and brilliant cultural era. And later on, when Egypt preserved Arab culture from the onslaughts of crusaders and Mongols, Cairo became the intellectual centre of the Arab world.

Despite varying phases of internal development, strong influences from the outside world and changes in the language, social structure, faith, art, economy and law, the continuity of Egyptian civilisation and culture can be traced in many fields throughout the Pharaonic, Greco-Roman, Coptic and Arab periods. Human thoughts and ideas assume a lasting shape in the form of the written word; their impact is enshrined on stone, papyrus, parchment, paper, wood and shards of all kinds. In its broadest sense literature is a part of this cultural continuity of Egypt's history, for books developed out of the papyrus roll to become parchment and paper codices written in many languages.

The Pharaonic Period

Egyptian Writing Utensils

The Egyptian scribes used brushes made of stems of reeds 1.5 to 2.5 millimetres thick cut to a length of 16 to 23 centimetres. They were beaten or chewed to pulp at one end and kept in a tubular receptacle. Ink, which has retained its pitch black colour surprisingly well over thousands of years, was made of carbon mixed with gum. For rubrics they also had red ink made of ochre and gum. Since the ink was in the form of a powdered pigment kept in a bag or on a palette, a small pot containing water for dissolving the ink also belonged to the scribe's equipment. The holder for the brushes, bag and palette were tied together. The scribe either carried his writing utensils in his hands or—if he needed his hands for other things —slung over his shoulder in such a way that the palette lay on his chest, ink bag and brush holder on his back.

Naturally, the writing utensils changed their form in the course of centuries. In ancient times a rectangular palette with two depressions for the red and the black ink was used. During the Fifth Dynasty of the Old Kingdom a shell was often used to dissolve the ink in. The shell could be attached by a loop in the same way as the palette. At the end of the Fifth Dynasty a new palette came into fashion. Instead of the old circular depressions, solidified red and black ink was glued to the upper part of the palette and the extended lower part had a covered slot where reed brushes were kept. In addition, a tassel was tied to the upper edge; it was probably used to erase errors, very much like a sponge attached to a slate. These new writing utensils which were much easier to handle were still used, with slight modifications, at the time of the New Kingdom.

The discovery of papyrus, the principal writing material, must have taken place during the dawn of Egyptian history, because the hieroglyphic sign of a roll, probably representing a papyrus roll, and that of a scribe's writing utensils already occur in the First Dynasty. The oldest (but unwritten) papyrus we know of was found in the tomb of Hemaka, an official of the First Dynasty, and the first written papyrus we know of dates back to the Fifth Dynasty. The term "papyrus" (our word "paper" derives from it) is probably of Egyptian origin. It is assumed that the term is to be translated as "the writing material of the king" and that this refers to the royal papyrus monopoly of the Ptolemies.

The papyrus (Cyperus papyrus, L.) is a plant growing in still waters and marshes and its triangular stalks can reach a height of three to six metres. In ancient times the plant grew all over the country, especially in the marshy districts of Lower Egypt, but today papyrus is only to be found in the Sudan and in Ethiopia. The ancient Egyptians used the plant for various purposes: the stems were made into sails, sandals, cloth, cords and

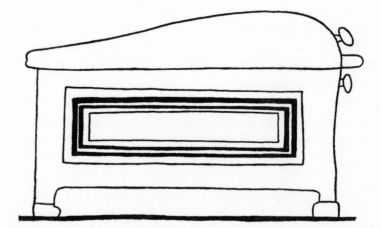

Receptacle for papyrus rolls: New Empire wooden chest.
Wall painting from the Tomb of Menena, Thebes

A drawing taken from a relief in the Tomb of Kaninisut
in Gîza, Vienna

mats; the plant was also used as the principal material in the construction of light skiffs. The account given by Pliny the Elder of the manufacture of writing material from the papyrus plant refers to the process followed in his own time; for earlier periods we have to rely on examination of pieces that have survived. The Egyptians themselves do not tell us anything about the subject. Among the many wall paintings in tombs we find scenes depicting the harvesting of papyrus, but no indication of the manufacture of writing material from it. It is assumed that it was worked as follows: the stems were cut into longitudinal strips, these were laid side by side to the required width, thus forming a layer across which another layer of shorter strips was laid at right angles. The whole was pressed, hammered and dried. The finished sheets were roughly one tenth of a millimetre thick, non-absorbent and flexible. Any roughness was levelled and the edges cut straight; to form a roll the sheets were joined together with paste, with about 20 sheets making up a roll. The scribe could then cut the roll or add further sheets as required. The longest roll known to us is 40 metres. New sheets were glued on with starch paste, leaving an overlapping strip between 1 and 2 centimetres

wide. As these joins were well pressed and levelled they did not interfere very much with the writing process. The degree of care exercised by the scribes differed, of course. A close examination reveals the difference between the gluing done by a craftsman and the less finished effort of the scribe himself. The sheets had a height of between 16 and 42 centimetres and the length of the sheets varied widely. Rolls were supplied in widths of between 42 and 47 centimetres and shortened by the scribe according to his purpose and wish.

The colour of papyri that have survived varies between yellow and darkest brown. One has to be very careful in judging the approximate age of a papyrus roll by its colour, because its condition depends upon the circumstances under which it was preserved. There are rolls of the same age whose colours range between yellow and dark brown. When new, the papyrus sheets were white or nearly white. White is the colour of the hieroglyphic sign for a papyrus roll in carefully drawn and painted inscriptions, and the statues of seated scribes hold papyrus rolls that have been coloured white. The Egyptians knew that papyrus yellowed with age. In two tombs of the New Kingdom, those of Thutmose III and Amenophis II, religious texts were inscribed on the walls in cursive book-hand hieroglyphs on a yellow-brownish background, representing the colour of a papyrus of venerable age.

Since papyrus was at all times an expensive material, palimpsests were often employed: used papyrus was wiped clean by the scribe and used again. This was also the reason why in schools limestone fragments and ostraca were used for calculations, sketches and other purposes. But these ostraca were also washed quite often and used again. Furthermore, small wooden tablets smoothed with a thin white layer of plaster were used for exercises and brief notes.

Leather was only seldom used as writing material. It was reserved for especially valuable or important texts such as official documents of the royal archives or for temple rituals. Papyrus rolls were kept in jars, wooden boxes or leather receptacles. Reliefs and paintings on the walls of tombs depict these boxes and leather receptacles. From the Fifth Dynasty onward scribes at work in chancelleries, in the fields or elsewhere are shown as well. We see them hard at work with their palette, reed brush and papyrus roll, with their various utensils and written and unwritten rolls spread around them. Pictures of the Old Kingdom show flat corded cases with rounded corners, but more often various kinds of leather containers (e.g. a long cylindrical case with cap top or a bag with a handle at the side) which were easier to transport than the wooden chests because they were lighter and less bulky. In the Middle Kingdom there were rectangular wooden chests, while in the New Kingdom wooden chests with rounded covers and short legs are found. In the Museum in Cairo there is a New Kingdom chest whose owner was a lady named Ijneferti. The chest has short legs, and the lid is painted with pictures probably relating to the papyrus rolls it once contained.

Hieroglyphic Writing

Formerly the opinion prevailed that Egyptian hieroglyphs were the last link of a longer chain of development. More recently we have discovered that this system appeared quite suddenly as a successful innovation at a certain time, although we cannot exactly determine the date. It is, of course, quite clear that such an invention did not occur spontaneously, but that it had an intellectual background. We can understand the reasons for this phenomenon when we take into consideration the period of its manifestation. It appeared at a time when the human race was beginning to think in terms of history and to widen its horizon beyond the narrow confines of the individual and his world. This gave rise to the need to record names and dates; the discovery of writing thus constitutes the beginning of Egyptian history. We find the oldest signs on cosmetic palettes from the beginning of the First Dynasty, and towards the end of the Second Dynasty the system was already fully developed.

We shall now look briefly at the structure of hieroglyphic writing. It is based on the use of pictures (ideograms) for words. Words like "mountain" or "house" are reproduced by their respective pictures. This procedure shows us the principle of picture writing not yet bound to a language, since these pictures could be read in all languages. Thus the real invention of writing consists in the introduction of phonetic signs reproducing a spoken language (phonograms). Egyptian was a language in which the roots of words were usually composed of consonants which might combine with any number of different vowel patterns, as well as suffixes and prefixes. Since only the consonants remained the same in different usages of the same root, the hieroglyph for that root came to be associated with the consonants only, leaving out the vowels. It was possible, for instance, to write all those words with the picture sign for basket ("nb") which had the same sequence of consonants, such as: "Lord", "everybody", "to swim". Here the sign represents consonants, not ideas (in the case of "nb" a sign for two consonants). It was thus possible to write all words which could not be expressed in the simple picture script: groups of abstract terms, adjectives, pronouns, particles, etc. As there was at least one sign for each of the 24 consonants, in the case of brief words consisting of one consonant and one vowel, it would have been possible to get rid of the whole ballast of complicated hieroglyphic writing comprising over 700 signs. It would have been possible to write practically everything with the aid of these signs, only adding signs to designate words belonging to a certain type or class (determinatives) for the sake of clarification. The Egyptians were aware of the potentialities of such a way of writing and they did use it, e.g. for writing foreign names, but they never practised it consistently.

Since a given sign might have several different sound values according to the word that was to be expressed, other signs were added to make sure that the reader understood what was meant. For this purpose one or more consonants of the intended word were repeated as phonetic signs after the ideogram. Thus the single

32,33
35,37

30,31

36

29

consonant sign for "b" was added after the sign for "nb". As mentioned above, determinatives were also used to define the meaning. In order to distinguish between hieroglyphs which could be understood both as ideogram and phonogram, the diacritical mark was used. Thus "nb" meaning "basket" was written with a diacritical sign and "nb" meaning "everybody" without.

As implied in the term itself, which is composed of two Greek words meaning "sacred" and "sculpture", hieroglyphs were above all used for inscriptions on monuments. They were used mainly for writing on wood and stone, and—as their monuments covered with inscriptions show—the Egyptians were at all times aware of the highly decorative value of their script. Even in the oldest period there was a cursive equivalent, known as hieratic script in which, as a result of the writing materials involved (reed brushes and papyrus), single signs were abridged and combined until they became unrecognizable. An even more abbreviated form of cursive writing known as demotic was used together with and often instead of the hieratic characters from the Twenty-sixth Dynasty on. As far as we know it was introduced originally for official records and later was used for literary and religious texts as well.

The Scribes

The profession of an official—of a "scribe" as the Egyptians called him—was at all times in Egypt deemed an ideal occupation worthy of the highest esteem. The scribe's profession was the basis for state administration—the intellectual elite of the country was recruited from *32,33* it. He who knew how to write could enter the "cursus honorum", attain the highest state appointments and *35,37* thus participate in government. The ramification of the administration, which from the early days of the Old

Kingdom expanded, absorbing more and more people, created an extremely self-assured class who, because of *30* their education and knowledge, regarded themselves as being above the masses of illiterates. They prided themselves in having access to higher education, to classical writings and to the doctrines of life and of knowledge of their ancestors and in enjoying material advantages and security as well as in not having to do any physical work. Intractable pupils were told in well-chosen words about the advantages of the scribe's profession: "As far as the scribe is concerned, whatever post he may occupy in the state, he will never be in need."

"Be a scribe, because your limbs are smooth and your hand fatigues easily. Then you will not burn out like a lamp (through work) like those whose limbs are exhausted, for indeed your bones are not those of a man... Your limbs are weak and your body is without strength. Decide to become a scribe—it is a fine profession suited to you. You will summon one, and thousands will answer your call. You will be free to come and go and not be yoked like an ox which is bartered. You will take precedence over others." Even princes and high officials were fond of having themselves represented in writing posture with *27,29* papyrus and brush or reading from an opened roll.

The establishment of schools is thought to have begun in the Middle Kingdom. In ancient times officials trained their successors by educating one or several chosen pupils in their own houses. Furthermore, there were the "court schools" where the local nobility, high officials, but also people from socially lower classes could send their sons to have them educated with the young princes. Those who enjoyed this honour regarded it as a special distinction, and the court looked with approval at these school friendships which served to link future high officials, the future holders of key positions in the administration, with the crown princes. From the Middle Kingdom onward schools existed in which several children were

Examples of writing
above: hieratic
below: demotic

taught the art of reading and writing together in one class. Lessons at the schools attached to temples were generally given outdoors. When excavating on the site of these "classrooms", large quantities of limestone fragments and other ostraca, which constituted the Egyptian schoolboy's copybooks, were found. On the other hand, pupils of the higher classes who had progressed further in the art of writing and were allowed to write on papyrus obtained the material they needed by washing old rolls and using them again. They also obtained writing material from the unused backs of old sheets or by cutting out blank spaces and gluing them together to form new rolls.

As far as the standard of education and what subjects pupils were taught are concerned, we are best informed about the New Kingdom. Once the fundamental elements of reading and writing had been learnt in the lower classes, succeeding time was spent in exercising spelling and improving handwriting by copying or taking down dictation. The pupil was expected to sharpen and form his intellect by reading and copying doctrines of life and knowledge. Since the Egyptians at all times esteemed the art of oratory, particular attention was given to the study of rhetoric. The future official was expected to be fluent and elegant in his speech, to be able to play on words and weave proverbs and quotations into his well-chosen and polished words. He had to know all the rules and forms of refined letter-writing as well as the complex, rigid phraseology of oral and written address. To this end the pupils had to copy model letters and chosen pieces of literature to prepare them later on "to speak to counsellors, to be familiar with the rules at court, to respond to a speech and to send an answer to a letter"; "to stand up at the place where there is dispute and to approach the place where there is discussion." Besides education in spelling and literature, Egyptian pupils had to learn mathematics and geometry and to strengthen their bodies through physical exercise. They had to obtain a certain knowledge of geography, to memorize the names of the towns, shrines, fortresses, mountains and provinces of Egypt and of regions known to the Egyptians at the time of the Empire, and to learn the spelling of these names by heart. There were lists of all these localities which had to be copied and memorized. To add to their geographical knowledge, to familiarize themselves with the correct way of writing foreign places and proper names and as a model of good and polished speech, pupils in the New Kingdom also used to read about the "literary controversy" which we know from the Papyrus Anastasi I. This is a letter written by the scribe Hori to another (probably imaginary) scribe,

in which he questions the other's claim to have visited various regions of the Near East, and to know them well. By giving detailed lists of localities and descriptions of landscapes Hori attempts to show that the other scribe really neither knew nor saw anything. His language is elegant and, despite its acerbity, never violates the rules of courtesy. "...So I write to thee to instruct thee, as a friend teaches one who is greater than himself to be an outstanding official... I speak to thee of another city abroad. Byblos is its name; what is it like—who is its goddess?... Come tell me about Beirut, and about Sidon and Sarepta. Where does the river of Litani flow? What is Uzu like? There is another city by the sea called the port of Tyre. Water is brought to it in boats, and it is richer in fish than sand... Come, set me on the road south of the region of Acco. Where does the Achshaph Road lead to? To the gates of what city? Pray tell me about the mountain of User! What kind of a peak does it have? Where is the mountain of Shechem?... If one travels to Idumaea whither does one turn one's face? Do not withhold thy knowledge; be our guide so that we may learn it!... Pray teach me concerning the appearance of Qena; acquaint me with Rehovoth; explain Beth-shan and Tirqa-el. How does one cross the ford of the River Jordan? Tell me how one can pass Megiddo, which lies above it, without hindrance... O, honoured scribe, Mahir cunning of hand," (the recipient of the letter is said to have assumed this title, which is the word for "express messenger" in the language spoken in Canaan); "foremost of the young soldiers, the first in the army, I describe to thee the countries bordering on the land of Canaan, but thou answerest me neither rightly nor wrongly; thou returnest me no reply!"

Above we mentioned the "doctrines of life" and before going any further we would like to return to this kind of literature since, according to everything we know, it constituted a major part of what was taught. One of the Egyptian teachers' main concerns was to mould the intellect and character and to educate the young to be useful and reliable members of society. To reach this goal, the texts of these maxims formed the basis of instruction and the pupils had to copy them and learn them by heart. These doctrines are instructions for living related to practice; based on observation of life and people, they provide a guide to correct behaviour. They teach when to speak and when to remain silent, they give recommendations for correct behaviour in the presence of the mighty and the humble, for righteous action before god and human beings—they therefore embrace all realms of human life. The oldest doctrine known is that of Diedefhor, a son of Cheops. It gives instructions for conducting one's life; for instance to marry early, to appoint one's house well, and to think in good time of building and furnishing one's tomb. The Maxims of Ptahhotep and Kagemni also date from the Old Kingdom; the Middle Kingdom gave us the Maxims of "Cheti, son of Duauf" (possibly read as "Dua-Cheti") and those of King Amenemhet; those of Ani and Amenemope are from the New Kingdom. To cite some brief extracts: "Then the vizier had his children (pupils) called to him after he had looked into the hearts of men and clearly perceived their character. Then he said to them: 'All that is said in this roll has to be understood just as I said it. Do not exceed the bounds of its instructions.' And at that they knelt down. They read it aloud as it had been written. It was more precious to them than anything else in their whole country and they moulded the rest of their lives accordingly" (from the epilogue to the Maxims of Kagemni).

Title and part of the prologue of Ptahhotep's precepts: "Treatise of the mayor of the capital and of the Vizier Ptahhotep under his Majesty King Asesin, may he live forever... the mayor of the capital and Vizier Ptahhotep says: 'O King, my Lord, age has come, old age descended on me... may this servant (myself) be permitted to have a staff to lean on in his old age (a pupil). I would like to tell him the words of those who were obedient to the advice of the ancestors, who once harkened unto the gods...!' The Divine Majesty said unto him: 'Educate him in the sayings of the past, may he be a model for the sons of the great, may he acquire obedience and all the righteousness of heart of the one who instructs him. Nobody was ever born a wise man.'" And from the precepts: "Do not be proud of your knowledge. Confer with the ignorant as with the wise—nobody can attain ultimate perfection and there are no artists whose mastery is complete. Good words are like hidden gems, but they can nevertheless be found amongst the maid-servants at their millstones!"

Although these precepts were not exclusively written for schoolboys we have, however, a specially compiled work for schools in the "Kemit" (completion, perfection), i.e. a real school and reading book which the boys had to copy and learn. It was probably compiled at the beginning of the Middle Kingdom and was still used for school lessons in the New Kingdom. As a kind of manual it contained roughly all the information which was important for the pupil—from formulas of polite written and oral address and model letters to the inevitable appeal to the pupil to be diligent and praise of the scribe's profession.

We already mentioned that the Egyptian script was not alphabetical writing—despite the signs for single consonants—but that there was a definite succession of signs for each word which the writer had to learn and know by heart. He therefore could not write a word correctly just by hearing it. He had to know the orthodox "spelling", i.e. the sequence of hieroglyphs demanded. Therefore, copying and dictation to practise what he had learnt were integral elements of Egyptian educational methods. We learn from texts that teachers used various disciplinary measures to educate their pupils. They tried to stimulate competition among them: "Surpass (thy classmates) so that thou may'st be sent on a mission." They warned and threatened them: just as it is possible to tame and train animals, it is also possible to subdue intractable pupils. But they also employed drastic measures, such as imprisonment: he who ignored all warnings and threats could well be put in the stocks where he had to remain motionless until he was willing to work. Judging from the texts, corporal punishment was frequently administered: " Do not be lazy for a single day, otherwise thou willst be beaten. The ear of a boy is on his back, he hears when he is beaten." "With the hippopotamus whip I will teach thy legs to idle around the streets!" However, most of the time the teachers issued admonitions. According to the frequency with which they occur in texts, it would seem that the pupils were exhorted without pause from morning till evening: "Thou pupil, do not be lazy or thou willst immediately be humbled! Do not devote thyself to dancing, lest thou be a failure! Write with thy hand, read with thy mouth and ask the advice of those who know more than thou." The pupil is forcefully confronted with the hard life of a peasant or soldier compared with that of the much-lauded scribe and scholar who has easy and pleasant work and enjoys a high standing, whose activities are useful, representing an eternal monument to himself: "Those learned scribes since the times of those who followed the gods, those who predicted the future, they are the ones whose names are immortal—although they passed away having completed their life's span and although their relatives have been forgotten... Gates that were erected at their tombs have perished. Their priests have departed, their sacrificial stones are covered with earth, their burial chambers forgotten. But their names are remembered because of the books they wrote, because their books are good, and the author will not be forgotten in all eternity. Decide to become a scribe so that thy name, too, will last forever...

"A man perishes, his body becomes dust, all his contemporaries are under the earth. But the book perpetuates his memory from mouth to mouth. A book is more useful than a house, or shrines in the west, it is more than a firmly built palace or memorial stone in a temple."

The Appearance of the Manuscripts

Only in a few cases can we determine the place and circumstances under which manuscripts now in our possession were found. For the majority of papyrus rolls information on these two points is either unreliable or completely lacking. The latter is mostly the case when papyri were purchased from Egyptian merchants who knew nothing about their origin or preferred to say nothing—in view of prospective future material from the same source or the risk of being associated with the marauders who plundered the tombs (an act forbidden by law); they had no scruples about dividing the papyri they found, thus increasing their number by tearing the rolls apart, even in the middle of a sheet.

Papyri have been found in tombs, but also, during the excavation of ancient cities, in temple archives and in houses (e.g. those of officials). During the excavation of the pyramid city of Sesostria II numerous rolls were found in temple archives; they consisted of administrative documents as well as literary, mathematical and medical texts. In a tomb of the Thirteenth Dynasty in Thebes a book chest with a painted cover was found. It contained a number of valuable texts, e.g. a papyrus devoted to geography, several medico-magical texts, a papyrus containing an ancient coronation festival play, fragments of the "Tale of Sinuhe", etc. And according to the finder of the Lansing Papyrus, a school writing exercise from the New Kingdom, he discovered it in a jar in a Theban tomb. In the vicinity of Saqqarah a jar was found containing one legal and one medical text. And it is believed that the papyrus containing the Amenemope Maxims was found together with other manuscripts in a wooden statuette of Osiris in a Theban tomb. Not very long ago a papyrus providing further evidence about an already known case of tomb robbery during the reign of Ramses IX came to light in a statuette in Brussels. In one of the Theban tombs native workers are supposed to have found a chest with several rolls, including the one with magic spells which has become known as the Harris Magical Papyrus.

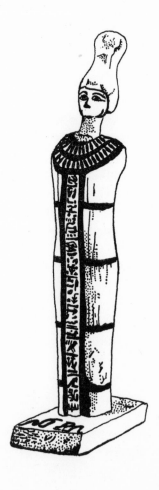

The Harris Papyrus I (today in the library of the British Museum No. 10053), one of the most magnificent Ramses manuscripts, was bought by the Englishman Harris, after whom it is named. According to the data given by the merchant who sold it to him it was hidden in the Theban necropolis and found in 1855. It is 40.5 metres long and 42.5 cms broad. The document records details of what Ramses III did for the temples during his reign. It was written by his successor, Ramses IV, after the murder of Ramses III.

The Ebers Papyrus (today in the University Library of Leipzig) was bought in 1873 by the Leipzig egyptologist Ebers in Luxor. It is alleged to have been found in a Theban tomb. From the calligraphical aspect it is probably the finest manuscript to survive from ancient Egypt. With a length of over 20 metres it is moreover the longest medical papyrus known to us and also the most important from the point of view of providing information about medicine in ancient Egypt. It contains prescriptions as well as extracts from different sources relating to all kinds of diseases.

The Edwin Smith Medical Papyrus, like the Ebers Papyrus with which it shows close similarity, was probably found in the Theban necropolis too, as both manuscripts appeared on the Egyptian market around 1865. Written somewhat earlier than the Ebers Papyrus, it is much shorter; it is only 4.70 metres long.

But in the majority of cases, as already mentioned, we do not know where the papyri were first found. One of these manuscripts, for instance, is the Westcar Papyrus (now in Berlin), which was written in the late Middle Kingdom. It gives an account of miraculous happenings at the court of King Cheops as a prelude to the equally miraculous story of the birth of the triplets who were destined to become the kings of the Fifth Dynasty. The Prisse Papyrus from the beginning of the Twelfth Dynasty is another case in point. It was purchased in Thebes by the French scholar Prisse d'Avennes and it can be assumed that it was also found there. In 1847 it was transferred to the Bibliothèque Royale in Paris. The papyrus contains two books—the latter part of the Instructions of Kagemni and the whole of the Maxims of Ptahhotep. Since the names of the authors are known from other Old Kingdom sources, it can be assumed that the text of the papyrus dates back to that time.

These brief examples will suffice to indicate where and under what circumstances papyri were found, and we will now deal with the appearance and arrangement of the writing on the papyrus rolls.

Despite its flexibility and elasticity papyrus was, even under the most favourable conditions, an extremely fragile material. Certain measures were necessary to prevent the exposed edges from fraying and tearing through continual use. These exposed edges along the sides were therefore reinforced by a protective strip 5 to 9 cms in width, or at least a corresponding margin was left blank. The same procedure was adopted for the top and bottom of the roll. This was done, not only for aesthetic reasons, but also as a practical measure.

If writing was not done in a standing position, it was done sitting down with crossed legs, and the papyrus was laid without any support on the stretched kilt. The roll was held at right angles to the body and was unrolled with the left hand and rolled up with the right. The beginning was thus on the right-hand side and writing was done from the right to the left. Until the Twelfth Dynasty writing was done from right to left in vertical lines, horizontal lines being only used for dates, headings or signatures. After the Twelfth Dynasty writing was done (from right to left) in horizontal lines, but one page was divided up into several columns. In certain texts writing was done backwards, i.e. single signs were written from right to left, but vertical lines (or columns) followed each other from left to right. In other manuscripts two columns were written alongside each other in such a way that in one the signs were written from left to right and in the other from right to left so that they "looked at each other". Administrative documents

Row of illustrations below the text of the Ramesseum Dramatic Papyrus

formed an exception; it was customary to hold them perpendicularly so that the lines ran parallel to the narrow side of the papyrus. The only known exception is thus all the more interesting. Since a Moscow papyrus containing an account of the voyage of Wenamum, i.e. a literary text, is written in this way, it can be assumed that it is an official report which the traveller wrote for some chancellery.

If the scribe had several sentences all beginning in the same way, he wrote this part once, leaving an empty space for the repetition in the following lines. Several other possibilities were found to avoid the repeated writing of such identical sequences. The sentence or part of the sentence which had to be repeated was written vertically in front of the horizontally written variations. Or it was written in a horizontal line above several vertical lines, even on top of two columns of vertical lines. The number of examples for the pattern of writing where identical parts of sentences recur—be it at the beginning, in the middle or at the end—could be enlarged considerably.

Aids for the separation of lines seldom occur; when they were used, they are to be found above the text, in between two or more lines or between vertical lines. Indenting at the beginning of a paragraph according to our usage was unknown. In Egyptian texts the first sign on a line is always above the first sign on the next line. The end of the line could be left blank for various reasons. The length of the line within a column was variable, as was the number of lines in a column. Thus the number of lines in the columns of the "Tale of Sinuhe" found in the Berlin papyrus varies between 13 and 17 in a page length of 16 cms, and in another Berlin papyrus (the "Eloquent Peasant") there are between 8 and 14 lines in one column in a page length of 16 cms. The numbering of lines or columns was

obviously not common; it is seldom found in the papyri known to us. The large Ebers medical papyrus in the University Library of Leipzig may be cited as example.

A seal or the title could be put on the outside of the roll. Occasionally the title of a papyrus was put on the chest in which it was kept. The British Museum has a faience ex libris bookplate of King Amenophis III and Queen Tiy on which is inscribed the "Book of the Sycamore and the Olive". It is assumed that this bookplate was once affixed to the chest in which this particular book was kept.

Where books were referred to in a text, longer titles were abbreviated. If a book had no title, the beginning of the text was cited. We know many titles without knowing anything about the books themselves. They are listed on papyri or on the walls of temples. Often the title of a book indicates that it was a collection—of songs, recipes, magic spells, mathematical problems, etc. An example of this is the funerary papyrus known as the "Book of Coming-Forth-by-Day". The individual sayings, recipes, etc. are separated by sub-titles, such as "Another exercise" (followed by a similar example). In the Maxims of Amenemope longer paragraphs are divided and enumerated by a word "ḥ.t."—"house"—which we translate as chapter.

The scribe used red ink, which he had in addition to black on his palette, to indicate titles, headings, the start of a new paragraph or other parts of the text deemed important. These rubrics were used according to customs and rules which are difficult to comprehend, as there was a wide area of permissible variation, and individual taste and the desire for a neat arrangement obviously played an important role. In certain cases some scribes wrote the beginning of every piece of the text, however small, in red at the expense of clarity; others hardly used any red, or used it only in insignificant places, and this, too, resulted in a confusing impression. In certain circumstances red was not used at all, because according to Egyptian belief red signified evil and violence.

Dates were also very often written in red. They are usually to be found in official documents, i.e. in reports, accounts, letters and the like, but also in pupils' manuscripts under the exercises to be done on one day. Dates were written according to a stereotype formula: "year X, season Y, day Z".

In several texts red dots separate paragraphs. The dots are generally called "verse points". Recent research work on Egyptian metrics reveals that these dots, apart from a few explainable errors, were really used to separate verses. Although metrical structure is indicated by verse dots or pointed writing in only a few texts, it has been proved that nearly all Egyptian texts are metrically arranged according to stress and not the number of syllables. The single verse has two or three stresses, rarely four.

Finally we must mention a punctuation sign which was also not used consistently. Written in red it denoted a pause, usually after longer paragraphs, in magic spells, love songs, hymns and school exercises and sometimes at the end of letters.

Now and then pupils corrected their work with red rather than black ink. Corrections were often inserted between the lines. In view of the many often glaring mistakes that can still be found in school exercises, it would appear that they were discovered by accident and then corrected by the pupils themselves. Apparently teachers did not bother to make written corrections of each pupil's exercises. They probably restricted themselves to the punishments already mentioned or to oral warnings. Sometimes signs in the text itself are repeated on the margins of school exercises. These were originally assumed to be teachers' corrections, but here, too, it was probably the pupil himself who quickly tried out some newly learned signs in the margin, before actually starting to write. It could happen that a scribe who was copying a text arrived at a place where the original showed a gap between two words or signs or where the text was illegible. He would then either leave a gap at this place, or write the words "found damaged".

At the end of a manuscript a note (colophon) was often added expressing thanksgiving that the task had been completed and that it corresponded to the original. Sometimes the scribe's name and the date of completion of the manuscript were added. An example of a concluding remark is quoted from the "Tale of Sinuhe": "It has been taken down from beginning to end as it was found written." This corresponds to the demand for accuracy formulated in Ptahhotep's Maxims: "Do not leave out a word, do not add one, put none in the place of the other." This maxim became a commandment not to change the words of the scriptures in the book religions like Judaism and Christianity. In Egypt itself, on the other hand, this was not a guiding principle—it was always possible to re-interpret and adapt passages.

Now and then (especially in religious writings) a note

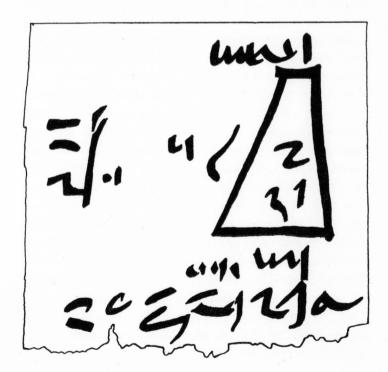

Illustration to the text of a mathematical papyrus, Moscow

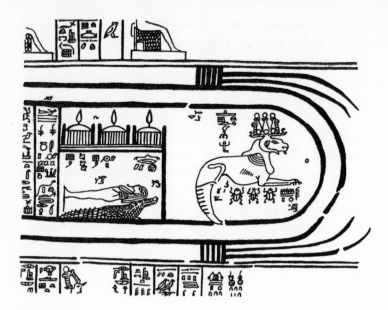

was added about the copied original, about its condition, age or the divine origin of the text. Such notes about divine origin, venerable age or remarkable circumstances under which it was found, as well as antedating and use of archaic language were made in order to distinguish the text from contemporary documents and increase its value.

We cannot leave the question of the appearance of the papyrus rolls without dealing with their illustration. We cannot determine at what time illustrations first appeared. The oldest illustrated Egyptian book we know of is the so-called Ramesseum Dramatic Papyrus, a coronation festival play contained in a manuscript from the end of the Middle Kingdom. However, we have reason to think that the papyrus is based on an older manuscript dating back to the Old Kingdom. This applies at least to the text; whether it also applies to the illustrations must remain an open question. Of the original manuscripts of the Old Kingdom only a few administrative documents are extant. Our knowledge about Old Kingdom "books" derives from copies made in later times. Thus the first illustrated book providing information about traditions whose origins are lost in the mists of history is the "Ramesseum Dramatic Papyrus" dating from the Middle Kingdom. With the beginning of the New Kingdom we enter the golden age of book illustration. In this period numerous and often outstandingly beautiful illustrated papyri for the dead and other manuscripts are witness to the high degree of perfection that had been attained.

Despite the gaps in our knowledge we can assume that in general the text was given priority over the illustrative picture. The "pyramid texts" with which from the reign of King Unas it was customary to adorn the walls of the

burial chambers and those of the passages leading to them do not have any illustrative additions. The need for illustrations was not felt, because the signs themselves were seen as pictures. The extent to which this was still the case at that time is shown by several instances where signs picturing living beings were mutilated for fear that the power of an image could endanger the dead. It was only later that it began to seem necessary to illustrate important aspects and pleasure was experienced in adding explanatory drawings or pictures. At a time when texts for the dead, originally the prerogative of the monarch, were available to everybody as a result of the "democratisation of the cult of the dead", the picture became a kind of substitute for reading, at least for the illiterate who could understand only the illustrations of their book of the dead. In this case illustrations fulfilled the same social function as the "Biblia pauperum" of the Middle Ages. Pictures were added to manuscripts not only because of the pleasure of ornamenting a book or out of consideration for the illiterate; there are also cases in which addition of illustrations can be explained by virtue of the magical powers they were considered to possess. There is, for instance, in the Book of the Dead, chapter 100, an instruction for the transfiguration of the dead one when he boards the boat of Re. The accompanying vignette is an illustration for an amulet: "To speak above this painted picture which is drawn on a clean sheet with fresh watercolours mixed with myrrh-water... When it is put on the neck of the transfigured one, he shall board the boat of Re." We see that the conception of the magic properties of images remained but in inverted proportions. The pictographs adorning burial chambers in the pyramids were once felt to possess a potent power that was feared. In later times the picture had to be animated by the magic of words in order to preserve its power, formerly taken for granted. The identity of picture-writing and what it stood for was lost.

A survey of the huge mass of extant papyri shows that those containing narrative literature, in which illustrations might be expected, do not contain any. The fact that narratives are not illustrated at all may probably be explained by virtue of the fact that surviving texts from the New Kingdom are all school exercises, written by pupils for others or for themselves. It is understandable that such manuscripts—which were meant only for private use in practising writing—did not include illustrations.

34, 39   Among illustrated papyri, texts taken from the Book
40, 43   of the Dead are the most important. This category also
41   includes the so-called guides for the journey to the hereafter and compilations from books of the underworld
42   (above all, "Amduat" and the "Gate Book"), as well as the mythological papyri. These differ from the books of the dead in so far as the illustrations outweigh the text in extent and significance, in some places reducing it to simple captions. The pictures thus attain a quite
40   different status and function. The "satirical papyri" in London, Cairo and Turin also consist of a series of pictures with written explanations. These papyri contain sequences of pictures with the various scenes explained in writing. They are interpreted as illustrations to fables and satires. Scientific literature, too, includes illustrated papyri: geographical-mythological texts, magico-medical and astronomical books. In such cases the purpose of the treatise in question, which may often have been produced in a number of copies, might have necessitated pictures. Study of the material (not fully listed here) shows that text and picture correspond only partially. The vignettes have often lost their original connections with the text, expecially if text and picture were done by different persons. A comparative study of the link between picture and book shows that two main forms emerged: illustrations as explanatory additions to the text and illustrations as the dominating element with brief explanatory captions.

Finally, a word about the choice and sequence of text and vignettes. Certain vignettes belonged to every chapter of the Book of the Dead. In general we find that every chapter—with slight variations—has its appropriate vignette. But it also happens that the respective picture is missing at a certain place or that pictures appear to which the corresponding text is missing. That is to say the Book of the Dead was embellished with certain pictures and it was left to the discretion of the artist to choose the ones he wanted for his papyrus. It can be assumed that for this purpose he had collections of vignettes for the Book of the Dead in the form of a sample book. As far as the procedure of illustrating books of the dead is concerned, we can ascertain that, in some cases at least, text and illustration were not done by the same person. It is easy to see in the case of some papyri that the vignettes were painted first and the text added afterwards, very often at the expense of its accuracy. In such papyri there is often no precise link between pictures and text which either had to be abridged if the vignettes did not leave enough space, or interrupted and continued in another place because the picture involved was too far away. There are also cases in which the scribe wrote the text without a break, regardless of the position of the vignettes, or in which he used a different version of the text, so that the link between text and picture was completely missing.

Because of the great quantity of extant papyrus rolls, which nevertheless form only a fraction of those existing in ancient times, the question arises as to how and where the Egyptians collected and arranged their books. The texts indicate that papyri were kept because we read that copying was necessary when the original had become worm-eaten. Two institutions could have served as depositories: the "mansion of books" and the "mansion of life". "Mansion of books" was the designation both for the archives where books were kept and an administrative office. In the temple of Horus at Edfu there is a small room near the court which was used as an archive. The walls show inscriptions concerning "many chests of books and large leather rolls". They included all the literature appertaining to a temple: liturgy for daily rites and feast days; manuscripts containing the building plans and instructions for the decorations on the walls of the temple; incantations and priestly lore but also documents relevant to the administration. The "mansion of life" was more than a library—it was a kind of university. Here books of all kinds were not only collected and classified, they were also written and handed down to the younger generation. It was the place where all branches of knowledge were cultivated and taught. The term "mansion of life" also indicated that its purpose was primarily the custodianship of religious texts and the celebration of rites connected with the preservation of the king's life and that of Osiris.   43

We are not able to say according to which principles libraries in the "mansion of books" and in the "mansion of life" were arranged. But we know, nevertheless, that the collected rolls were listed in catalogues, according to their content, and kept in chests (or other receptacles) on which a tablet with the titles of the books could be fastened or whose covers bore paintings indicating the content of the rolls.

It is very doubtful whether any kind of book trade existed in ancient Egypt, because all the prerequisites were lacking. The broad mass of the people did not know how to read or write and had to be satisfied with listening. Oral transmission through a "story teller" was an ancient custom in the Orient and is still practised very widely. The small number of those who were not illiterate copied the books they needed themselves. Tem-

ples and the administration had their own scribes who produced the required manuscripts and documents. If one of the literate wanted to possess a certain book, he copied it. Only the funeral papyri were written as articles of trade. There are even papyri in which the place for the name was left blank to be filled in later. A close look shows that the name of the owner was sometimes inserted by another scribe at a later stage. Such cases justify the assumption that funeral papyri were not only written to order, but that a large number was kept in stock for trade purposes. For the illiterate, too, wanted to possess this book which guaranteed protection against the dangers of the hereafter in order to add it to their tomb furnishings.

Captions to the Illustrations

10 *Receptacle for papyrus rolls:* New Kingdom wooden chest. Wall painting from the Tomb of Menena. Thebes. Tomb No. 69; painted on plaster; Eighteenth Dynasty, about 1420 B.C.

11 *Receptacles for papyrus rolls: bags and corded boxes.* From a relief in the Tomb of Kaninisut in Gîza, Vienna, Kunsthistorisches Museum; limestone; Fifth Dynasty, about 2500 B.C.

13 *Examples of writing:* hieratic (above) and demotic (below). Twentieth Dynasty hieratic writing (about 1160 B.C.) from the Abbott Papyrus 5, 1—3. G. Möller, Hieratische Lesestücke, Heft 3, Berlin 1961, page 20. Demotic writing of the late period from the "Demotic Chronicle" (Pap. 215 of the Bibliothèque Nationale Paris) 6, 1—3. W. Spiegelberg, Die sogenannte Demotische Chronik, Leipzig 1914, Plate VI

16 *Papyrus roll (Book of the Dead) with title, found in a wooden Osiris statuette.* New York, Metropolitan Museum of Art. Thebes; Twenty-first Dynasty, about 1000 B.C., H. E. Winlock, The Egyptian Expedition 1929—1930, The Museum's Excavations at Thebes, Bulletin of the Metropolitan Museum of Art, Sect. II, New York, Dec. 1930, Fig. 26, 27

17 *Row of illustrations below the text of the Ramesseum Dramatic Papyrus.* Thebes; Twelfth Dynasty, about 1700 B.C. K. Sethe, Dramatische Texte zu altägyptischen Mysterienspielen, Untersuchungen zur Geschichte und Altertumskunde Ägyptens, Leipzig 1928, Plate 16

18 *Mutilations of signs in the Pyramid Texts 1837c:* K. Sethe, Die altaegyptischen Pyramidentexte, Vol. II, Leipzig 1910, Spr. 650 (conclusion)

19 *Illustration to the text of a mathematical papyrus.* Moscow, State Museum of Fine Arts. Thebes; Twelfth Dynasty,

about 1700 B.C. W. W. Struve, Mathematischer Papyrus des Staatlichen Museums der Schönen Künste in Moskau, Quellen und Studien zur Geschichte der Mathematik, Vol. 1, Berlin 1930, Plate 29

20 *Vignette from the Fayyum geographical papyrus* (section). In this geographical-mythological papyrus of the Ptolemaic period, illustrated with numerous finely drawn pictures of the gods, Fayyum, the seat of the cult of Suchos, is elevated to the country's religious centre, where all the major gods have temples. This section shows Suchos on the left, carrying the body of Osiris on his back; on the right, Amon with the body of a lion, crocodile's tail and the head of a ram, wearing the Atef crown; Fayyum; late period. R.V. Lanzone, Les Papyrus du Lac Moeres, Turin 1896, Plate VII

25 *Hesire wooden tablet* (section). The tablet shows Hesire seated before the offering table. Slung over his shoulder are his writing utensils consisting of palette, ink bag and brush holder. Egyptian Museum, Cairo. 1.15 m long, 0.08 metres thick. Tomb of Hesire in Saqqarah, Mastaba A 3; Fourth Dynasty, about 2270. L. Borchardt, Denkmäler des Alten Reiches im Museum von Kairo, Part I, No. 1426, Berlin 1937 General Catalogue

26 *Writing utensils—reed brush holder, ink bag and palette.* Replica of writing utensils from the Old Kingdom. The first palettes consisted of a small board with two depressions or ink wells for red and black ink. Attached to it was the little bag with a supply of solidified ink. It could be closed by drawing together the cord threaded through it. Staatliche Museen zu Berlin, Ägyptisches Museum

26 *Instrument for smoothing papyrus.* Egyptian Museum, Cairo, Cat. No. C 69,057a, J 39,785. Grey stone; 9.5 × 55 cms. Middle Kingdom

26 *Brush holder with scrolls at one end*. Egyptian Museum, Cairo, Cat. No. I 43,174. Hollow reed, Height: 35.5 cms. Deir el Bakhit (Gournah); New Kingdom, Eighteenth Dynasty.

26 *Scribe's palette made of wood and reeds* with two depressions for various colours and a third for reed brushes. Egyptian Museum, Cairo, Cat. No. C 69001. Wood and reed; length: 36.2 cms, width: 5.2 cms. Middle Kingdom

27 *Statue of Neferefre in the posture of a scribe;* his name is inscribed on his kilt, between his hands. Ägyptisches Museum, Leipzig, Cat. No. 2687. Red granite with traces of colour, height: 39 cms. Gîza; Sixth Dynasty, about 2300 B.C. H. Etzoldt-D. Müller, Ägypten, Leipzig 1960, Plate 15

28 *Ostracon containing an account for bread and beer* in hieratic writing. Ägyptisches Museum, Leipzig, Cat. No. 3961. Limestone; 13×9 cms. Deir el Medineh; Nineteenth Dynasty, about 1310 B.C. J. Cerny, Catalogue des ostraca hiératiques non littéraires de Deir el Médineh, Documents de Fouilles, Vol. 3, Cairo 1935, No. 29, Plate 8

28 *Papyrus roll with Amduat texts*, the property of a certain Horus-em-Chemmis. Staatliche Museen zu Berlin, Papyrus-Sammlung, P 3001. 7.36×0.34 metres. Twenty-first Dynasty, about 1000 B.C.

29 *Statuette of a scribe facing the god Thoth in the shape of a pavian*. Staatliche Museen zu Berlin, Ägyptisches Museum, Cat. No. 20,001, 1. Slate; pedestal: wood, about 12.7 cms in length. Height of the group: 9.5 cms. Eighteenth Dynasty, about 1420 B.C. A. Hermann, Ägyptische Kleinkunst, Berlin 1940, page 59

29 *Wooden tablet from the Tomb of Hesire in Saqqarah* (section). The hieroglyphic signs are not yet arranged in regular lines. But the craftsmanship with which the individual hieroglyphs have been carved clearly demonstrates the expressive and decorative character of ancient Egyptian writing. Egyptian Museum, Cairo. Wood, height: 1.15 metres; 0.11 metres thick. Tomb of Hesire in Saqqarah, Mastaba A 3; Fourth Dynasty, about 2720 B.C. L. Borchardt, Denkmäler des Alten Reiches im Museum von Kairo, Part I, No. 1427, Berlin 1937 General Catalogue

30 *Fragment of a Theban wall painting*. Gooseherds bringing their flock to a scribe. To the left, the scribe with palette, unrolled papyrus, book chest and a sack for the rolls. British Museum, London, Cat. No. 37978. Painting on plaster. Thebes; Eighteenth Dynasty, about 1400 B.C. A. Champdor, Die altägyptische Malerei, Leipzig 1957, page 131

31 *Wall painting from the Tomb of Menena*. Scribes noting the amount of corn delivered. Thebes. Tomb of Menena (Tomb No. 69), Painting on plaster, Eighteenth Dynasty, about 1420 B.C. A. Champdor, Die altägyptische Malerei, Leipzig 1957, page 167

32 *A relief from an Old Kingdom mastaba* (section). On the lower row a scribe with palette and reed brush noting weights. Egyptian Museum, Cairo, Cat. No. 1534. Limestone with traces of colour, width of the tablet: 2.36 metres. Saqqarah, Mastaba D 2; Fifth Dynasty, about 2500 B.C. L. Borchardt, Denkmäler des Alten Reiches im Museum von Kairo, Part I, No. 1534, Berlin 1937 General Catalogue

33 *Relief from the Tomb of Kaninisut*. On the left, Kaninisut with his son; on the right in three rows, scribes with brushes, palettes, rolls and various kinds of receptacles for books. They are presenting Kaninisut with lists of the tribute and accounts from his endowments. Kunsthistorisches Museum, Vienna, Cat. No. 4948. Limestone with traces of colour. Gîza, Tomb of Kaninisut; Third Dynasty, about 2500 B.C.

34 *Two pages of text with vignettes from Hunefer's Book of the Dead*. Left: At the entrance to the tomb ritual ceremonies designed to open the mouth of the mummy are performed. Right: a) Figures of the dead entering and leaving the hereafter. b) The dead playing a board game. c) The Ba, or soul of the dead, above the entrance to the tomb. d) Worship of the two lions embodying yesterday and tomorrow. British Museum, London, Cat. No. B. M. 9901.5 Papyrus; 38.5 cms wide. Thebes; Nineteenth Dynasty, about 1310 B.C. E. A. Wallis Budge, The Book of the Dead. Facsimiles of the Papyri of Hunefer, Anhai, Kerasher and Netshemet, London 1899, Papyrus of Hunefer, Plates 7 and 8

35 *Relief from the Tomb of Ti depicting a chancellery*. The scribes are noting deliveries with styles on papyri. One of them is leaning forward attentively with a fresh papyrus roll in his hand. Section. Saqqarah, Tomb of Ti. Limestone. Fifth Dynasty, about 2400 B.C. G. Steindorff, Das Grab des Ti, Veröffentlichungen der E. v. Sieglin Expedition II, Leipzig 1913, Plate 85

36 *Book Chest with painted cover, the property of Ijneferti*. Egyptian Museum, Cairo, Journal d'entrée No. 27271, Cat. No. 5227. Painted wood; 32×30 cms. Thebes. Tomb No. 11 (Tomb of Sn-ndm in Deir el Medineh); Nineteenth or Twentieth Dynasty. A. Hermann, Buchillustrationen auf ägyptischen Bücherkästen, MDAIK 15, 1957, page 113 and following, Plate 14,1

37 *Relief from the Tomb of Mereruka*. Local officials are brought before the authorities for collection of taxes. On the left is the official scribe; kneeling in the middle are three of the men in arrears with their tax payments and a fourth is being beaten. Saqqarah, Tomb of Mereruka. Limestone, Sixth Dynasty, about 2400 B.C.

37 *Page of text from the Harris Papyrus I*. The plate depicts the 79th and last sheet of this roll, one of the finest Egyptian papyri. The text, written in a particularly clear hand, describes the peaceful and flourishing state of the country under the rule of Ramses III and closes with a prayer for his successor and heir to the throne. British Museum, London, Cat. No. B. M. 10053. Papyrus; 42.5 cms

wide. Thebes; Twentieth Dynasty, about 1160 B.C. S. Birch, Facsimile of an Egyptian Hieratic Papyrus, London 1876, Plate 79.

38 *Vignette from the Harris Papyrus I.* In the first of the three large coloured vignettes found in the papyrus, Ramses III is depicted bringing offerings to the Theban triad Amon, Mut and Khonsu; the following text gives an account of endowments for their temples. British Museum, London, Cat. No. B.M. 10053. Papyrus; 42.5 cms wide. Thebes; Twentieth Dynasty, about 1160 B.C. S. Birch, Facsimile, Plate 2.

39 *Text and vignette from the Book of the Dead of Ani.* The papyrus of Ani and that of Hunefer are undoubtedly two of the finest of the large number extant in this category. The depicted scene (from the 175th chapter) portrays the climax and crucial moment on entering the underworld. Ani and his wife are led into the presence of Osiris and the other gods to face judgement on the conduct of their lives. The dead man's heart is placed on the scales by the god Anubis while the feather or image of Ma'at (Truth) is put in the other pan of the balance. To the right of the balance stands the scribe Thoth who acted as recorder; beside him is the "devourer" to whom the dead man's heart was thrown if his evil actions outweighed his good ones. British Museum, London, Cat. No. B. M. 10470.3. Papyrus; 27.6 cms wide. Thebes; Eighteenth Dynasty, about 1400 B.C. E. A. Wallis Budge, The Papyrus of Ani, Vol. I, London 1913, Plate 3

40 *Text and vignette from the Book of the Dead of Anch-ef-en-Khonsu.* The vignette shows the owner of the funerary papyrus bringing offerings to Re-Horakhte. Staatliche Museen zu Berlin, Papyrus-Sammlung P 3013 A. Papyrus; 25 cms wide. Sammlung d'Athanasi; Twenty-first Dynasty, about 1000 B.C.

40 *The Cairo "Satirical" Papyrus.* The delicate coloured drawings depict a lady rat holding a goblet on the left. Her hair is being dressed by a cat standing behind her while another cat is giving her an unrecognizable object. In the second scene, a rat baby is being looked after by a cat nurse who is followed by another cat carrying a large fan. In the next picture a jackal is carrying a vessel on a pole, while a cow lying in a byre receives the contents of the second vessel, carried by another jackal, to drink. Egyptian Museum, Cairo. Papyrus: 12 cms wide, total length 55 cms. Tanis; Twenty-second Dynasty, about 800 B.C. E. Brugsch-Bey, Ein neuer satyrischer Papyrus, ZÄS 35, 1897, page 140 and following, Plate 1.

41 *Guide for the journey to the hereafter of Amun-em-uja* section. The dead man's heart is called for (see Chapter 30 of the Book of the Dead). Facing him, from right to left: winged cobra with the beard of a god (guardian of the underworld), personification of Ma'at, the phoenix, scarab, heart scarab engraved with a passage from Chapter 30 of the Book

of the Dead, goddess of the Theban necropolis. Staatliche Museen zu Berlin, Cat. No. P. 3127. Papyrus; 23 cms wide, total length 1.73 metres. Twenty-first Dynasty, about 1000 B.C. S. Morenz, Altägyptischer Jenseitsführer, Papyrus Berlin 3127, Leipzig 1964

42 *Amduat Papyrus, the property of a certain Amenophis* (section). The Book of Amduat ("about that which is in the underworld") belongs to the category of guides to the hereafter. It describes the journey of the sun through the realm of the underworld during the twelve hours of darkness. The part depicted here shows the sun-god in the tenth hour of his journey through the underworld. Staatliche Museen zu Berlin, Cat. No. 3005. Papyrus; 0.39 ms wide, total length 2.36 metres. Minutoli Collection, Twenty-first Dynasty, about 1000 B.C.

42 *Mythological papyrus of an Amon priestess* (section). The dead woman brings offerings to Osiris, behind whom stand Isis and Nephthys. Egyptian Museum, Cairo, Cat. No. C. 2512. New Kingdom Papyrus.

43 *Papyrus of the Book of the Dead.* Text with vignette. Staatliche Museen zu Berlin. Cat. No. P 10466. Papyrus; 25 cms wide, total length 93 cms. Late period

43 *Vignette from the Salt Papyrus 825.* In the Salt Papyrus 825 we have a hieratic illustrated ritual book of the late period. The rites described in the book took place in the "Mansion of Life" and served the conservation of life and the protection of the king and Osiris. The text and the accompanying vignettes in the reproduction deal with the "rites of house opening" performed by Shu. The naos is opened and the new statuette of Osiris set. The custodianship of the Osiris statuette simultaneously served the safety of the king, whose security was a necessity, guaranteeing the maintenance of the universe and the continuity of life. British Museum, London, Cat. No. B.M. 10051,9 Papyrus; 18 cms wide. Memphis, late period. Ph. Derchain, Le Papyrus Salt 825 (B. M. 10051), rituel pour la conservation de la vie en Égypte, Académie royale de Belgique, Mémoires, Vol. 58, Brussels 1965, Figs. XIX and XX.

44 *Ex libris bookplate of King Amenophis III and Queen Tiy.* British Museum, London, Cat. No. 22878, R. 2292. Faience; 6.2×3.8 cms. Amarna; Eighteenth Dynasty, about 1400 B.C. H. R. Hall, An Egyptian Royal Book-plate, JEA 12, 1936, page 30 and following

44 *Page of text from the Sallier Papyrus II.* This hieratic papyrus, in which verse dots occur, includes the teachings of Dua-Cheti. A second copy is extant in the Anastasi Papyrus VII. In the reproduced text the advantages of a scribe's profession are extolled by describing the hard work performed by a mason. British Museum, London, Cat. No. B.M. 10182. Papyrus; 21.5 cms wide. Twentieth Dynasty, about 1180 B.C. E. A. Wallis Budge, Facsimiles of Egyptian Hieratic Papyri in the British Museum, London 1923, Plate 71

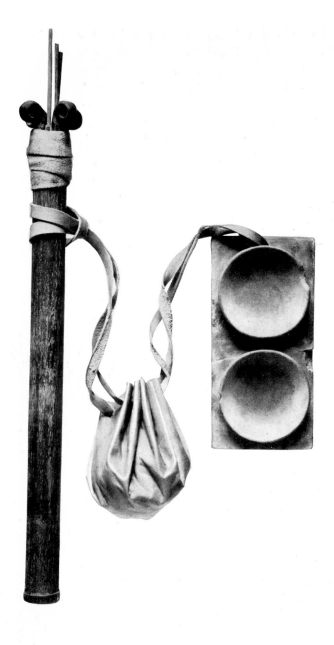

25 Hesire wooden tablet, section, Cairo

26 Writing utensils—reed brush holder, ink bag and
   palette, Berlin
   Instrument for smoothing papyrus, Cairo
   Brush holder with scrolls at one end, Cairo
   Scribe's palette made of wood and reeds, Cairo

27 Statue of Neferefre in the posture of a scribe, Leipzig

28 Ostracon containing an account for bread and beer, Leipzig
   Papyrus roll with Amduat texts, Berlin

29 Statuette of a scribe facing the god Thoth in the shape
   of a pavian, Berlin
   Hieroglyphic signs on a wooden tablet from the Tomb
   of Hesire in Saqqarah, section, Cairo

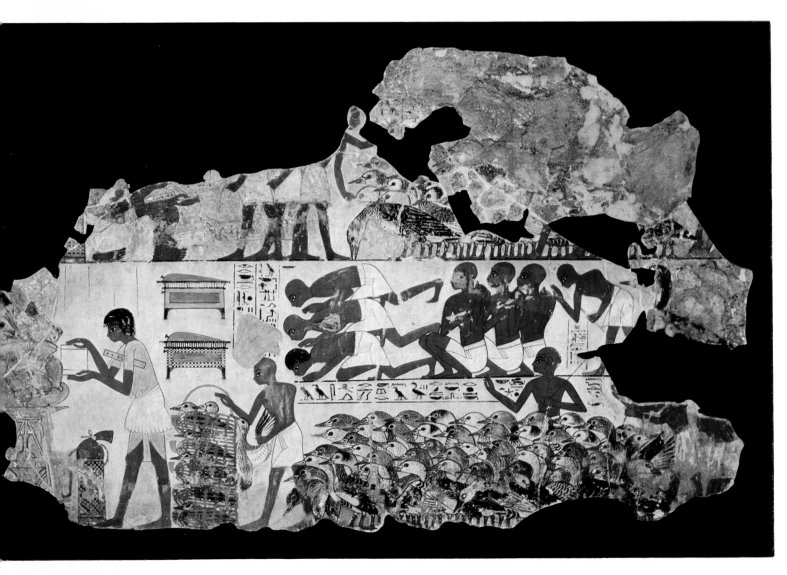

A relief from an Old Kingdom mastaba,
section, Cairo

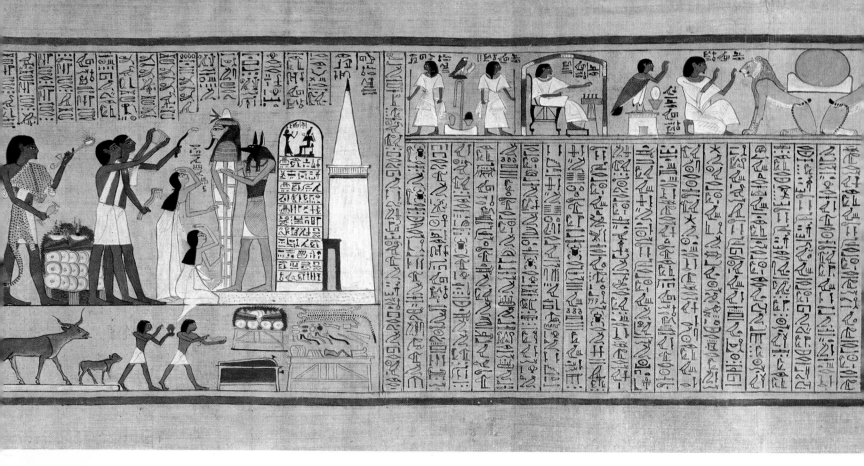

Two pages of text with vignettes from Hunefer's Book
of the Dead, London

36 Book chest with painted cover, the property of Ijneferti,
 Cairo

37 Relief from the Tomb of Mereruka, Saqqarah
 Page of text from the Harris Papyrus I, London

Text and vignette from the Book of the Dead of Ani, London

Text and vignette from the Book of the Dead
of Anch-ef-en-Khonsu, Berlin
The Cairo "Satirical" Papyrus, Cairo

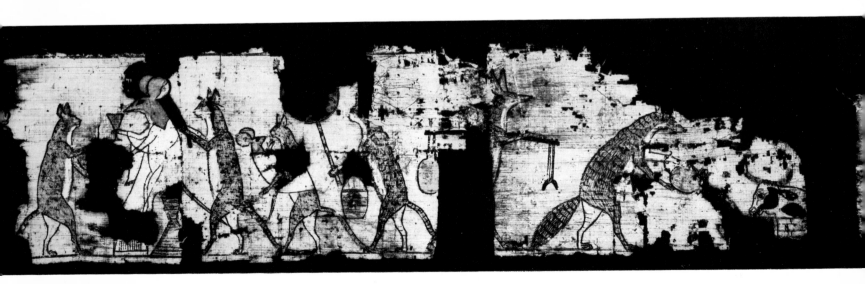

40

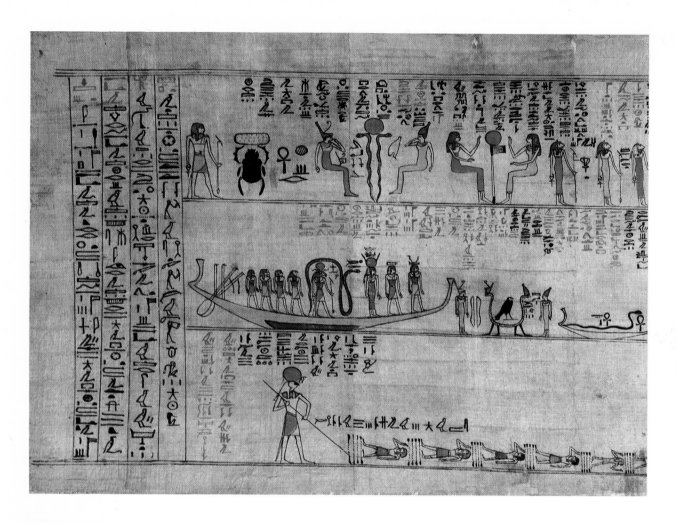

Amduat Papyrus, the property of a certain Amenophis, section,
Berlin
Mythological papyrus of an Amon priestess, Cairo

42

Papyrus of the Book of the Dead, text with vignette, Berlin
Vignette from the Salt Papyrus 825, London

Ex libris bookplate of King Amenophis III and Queen Tiy, London
Page of text from the Sallier Papyrus II, London

The Greco-Roman Period

Excavations and Finds

For a time of about a thousand years, from the conquest of Egypt by Alexander the Great, 332 B.C., until the beginning of Arab rule in the middle of the 7th century A.D., the official language of the country on the Nile was Greek. With the exception of a few Latin texts it was the language of official documents and of the Greek and hellenized upper classes under the rule of the Ptolemies and the Roman emperors. Among the people and the priesthood the Egyptian language was still in general use—demotic in its final written and spoken phase, followed by Coptic. Egyptian texts, both literary and of an official nature, survived until the Roman Empire, and ancient philosophy was preserved, even though it underwent a transformation. Letters and documents of all kinds were still written in the native language and form. But the overwhelming majority of the thousands of written testimonies to this epoch, found on papyri, parchment or ostraca, are in Greek, providing a clearer and more detailed picture of culture, society, economy, religion and law over a whole millennium than has survived from any other period of antiquity. Greek manuscripts, sometimes preserved in their entirety, but more often in the form of fragments, can be found in nearly all the world's major museums, libraries and collections. They have resulted in the development of papyrology as a special discipline of classical philology; scholars of many countries engaged in these studies constantly enlarge our knowledge of the history of Egypt during these thousand years through their publications and interpretations of this mass of written material.

Leaving aside the sensational discovery—only a part of which has been properly read—of 800 charred papyrus rolls which were found in 1752 in a house of an Epicurean philosopher during the excavation of the town of Herculaneum that was buried by the Vesuvius eruption in 79 A.D., it may be stated that all ancient papyri, parchments, ostraca and remainders of other writing material (with the exception of a few texts from Palestine and Mesopotamia) originated in Egypt, where they were preserved for coming generations in tombs and settlements, in particular at the edge of the desert, in the dry sand during thousands of years.

The deciphering of the so-called Charta Borgiana, a document roll in Greek cursive letters containing an account of compulsory labour recruited from the Fayyum village of Ptolemy Hermu for work on an irrigation project near Thebes in 192 A.D., may be considered as the beginning of scholarly interpretation of Greek papyri. The purchaser of the roll, Niels I. Schow, a Dane, performed a signal service in publishing the document. He presented the roll—now in the Vatican Museum—to Cardinal Stefano Borgia in 1778. But it was only as a result of Napoleon's Egyptian campaign and the subsequent brief occupation of the country (1798—1801) that the valley of the Nile was discovered by scholars; first by Frenchmen who collected the results of their research work—under the direction of E. F. Jemard—in a monumental work "Description de l'Egypte" which was published between 1809 and 1817. Soon scholars and travellers from all over Europe followed in their footsteps. The famous tri-lingual Rosetta stone, found in 1802, was the point of departure for an authentic decipherment of hieroglyphs, in which the young Frenchman Jean François Champollion was finally successful 20 years later. Egyptian antiquities were collected in Paris, London, Berlin, Turin, Leyden and Vienna, and scholars like Böckh, Droysen, Forshall, Leemans, Peyron, Brunet de Presle and others published the first important editions of Greek papyri.

These documents, many of which originated in Ptolemaic times, were purchased in Egypt and thus came to Europe. It was only in the middle of the 19th century that, due to Mariette's activities, systematic excavations were conducted in the big Serapeum of Memphis, where important fragments of literary texts were soon found. The first two rolls with Hyperides' speeches were thus handed over to the British Museum in London, verses by the early Greek lyric poet Alcman were given to the Louvre, and fragments of Homer's epics went to various museums and collections. In the seventies of the previous century investigation began on the rubbish heaps in the neighbourhood of ancient settlements where the indigenous peasants had long been accustomed to take compost (sebakh) for fertilizing their fields. Here, quantities of manuscripts, Arabic, Coptic and many Greek papyri of Byzantine times were found. Thousands of manuscripts were discovered especially in ancient cities like Arsinoe in Al Fayyum, Heracleopolis and Hermopolis; they were mostly acquired by London, Paris, and above all by Vienna, where they constituted the basis for Archduke Rainer's famous collection. About ten years later the second important finds in Al Fayyum, this time in Djeme, the ancient Soknopaiu Nesos, produced a rich yield, most of which was acquired by Berlin. At this time large fragments of Christian Apocryphal texts were found in Panopolis (Akhmim) and a long roll with Hyperides' speeches was acquired by the British Museum. In the same year, 1888, the British Museum acquired, with Aristotle's "Constitution of Athens", published in 1891 by F. G. Kenyon, and with the "Mimiambi" by Herodas, the most important finds of this period. It was also in 1891 that J. P. Mahaffy published the first larger edition of documents found with burial wrappings of the early Ptolemaic times. These finds were made in the course of several excavations under the direction of Sir Flinders Petrie in 1883/4 in Tanis, in 1889 in Hawara and in 1890 in Ghurab.

In the last decade of the 19th century the first volumes of the great series of Greek documents and literary texts appeared; these supply scholars with a huge mass of research material. Some well-known examples are the "Berliner Griechische Urkunden" (since 1892), the "Catalogue of Greek Papyri in the British Museum" (since 1893), and in particular the immense and still incomplete publication of "The Oxyrhynchus Papyri" (since 1898). The "Berliner Klassiker Texte" started with the publication of the Didymus commentary on Demosthenes' speeches (1904) and the anonymous commentary to Plato's "Theaetetus" (1905).

Vast excavation activities towards the end of the century resulted in the most important finds in Al Fayyum, Abu Sir, Abu Sir el-meleq, el-Hiba, Oxyrhynchus, Hermopolis, Aphrodito, Thebes, Edfu, Syene and on the Island of Elephantine. In 1895 the British Egypt Exploration Society (originally called the Egypt Exploration Fund) had acquired sufficient financial backing to undertake active and systematic excavations, especially under the direction of B. P. Grenfell and A. S. Hunt. Many sites were excavated at Karanis (Fayyum), but above all in Oxyrhynchus, where an amazingly rich yield of texts of all kinds was brought to light. Among the thousands of manuscripts the famous "Sayings of Jesus" were found here in 1897 as well as New Testament texts and masses of fragments of rolls and codices, including large numbers of previously unknown literary works of the early classical and Hellenist Greek periods. One year before, a large roll containing fragments of poems by the Greek poet Bacchylides had been acquired by the British Museum.

The first German excavations directed by U. Wilcken and H. Schäfer took place in Heracleopolis, and although some important material was found in 1898, the papyri were destroyed by a fire in the port of Hamburg. Fortunately, Wilcken was able to publish the copies of the texts he had made in Egypt. At the turn of the century Grenfell and Hunt made important finds at Tebtunis (southern Fayyum) where they discovered a cemetery of sacred crocodiles from Ptolemaic times; it yielded wrappings made from used papyri – documents originating from the official archives of Tebtunis. In a tomb near Abu Sir, L. Borchardt, the German architect and egyptologist, found one of the oldest Greek literary papyri, with large parts of the "Persians" by Timotheus of Miletus (about 400 B.C.), a nomos with cithara accompaniment which probably dates back to the last third of the 4th century B.C. It was also Borchardt who was able to acquire for Berlin 62 in Abu Sir el-meleq the famous coffin wrappings of documentary material of the late Ptolemaic and Augustan 62 period. Excavations under the direction of G. Rubensohn and F. Zucker in Hermopolis (1904) and on Elephantine (1906 and 1907) were equally successful. Besides the historically important Aramaic texts of the Jewish colony from the 5th century B.C., found in a closed earthenware receptacle next to other texts of the early Ptolemaic period, the oldest dated Greek original document, the marriage contract of 311/10 B.C., was discovered. It is now 63 one of the most precious texts of the papyri collection in the State Museums of Berlin. Later German excavations under the direction of F. Zucker in Al Fayyum (especially in Philadelphia) also brought manifold documentary material to light. But material purchased by F. Zucker and W. Schubart in the years before the First World War produced an even richer yield. Among these was the important "Gnomon of the Idios Logos", a manual for 64 the administration of the revenues of this central finance institution, dating back to about the middle of the 2nd century A.D.

However, the most important find of these years was made in 1915 in Philadelphia, when the archives of Zenon were discovered. He was the official representative and administrator of Apollonius, the powerful finance minister under Ptolemy II. The Museum in Cairo acquired the larger part of these documents. They are the most comprehensive Egyptian archives we know of and provide excellent information about a vast agricultural operation 65 in the middle of the 3rd century B.C.

After the First World War, too, primarily French and Italian, and also to an increasing extent American, institutions and scholars continued excavations in Egypt with considerable success, but the golden age of discovery of texts of the first importance seemed to be over, at least for the time being. Nevertheless in 1930, C. Schmidt, a Coptologist, was successful in acquiring several Coptic papyri codices from Al Fayyum for the Berlin Museums, as well as the Dublin Chester Beatty collection. These books, originally nine in number, were in an appalling condition, having been continually exposed to humidity. After their expert restoration by Dr. H. Ibscher and his son Dr. R. Ibscher, they proved to be a sensational discovery consisting of writings by Mani, the Iranian founder of Manichaeism.

After the Second World War the discovery of 13 Coptic-Gnostic papyrus codices at Nag Hammadi (1946), the ancient Chenosboscion, created as much sensation as the acquisitions and publications of the Bodmer Library in Cologny, Geneva. Among its precious possessions is the "Dyscolus", the first completely preserved comedy by the Attic poet Menander in a papyrus codex of the 3rd century A.D., as well as large fragments of two other plays by the same author and excellently preserved early texts of the Old and the New Testament in Greek and Coptic.

At many places excavations have started again and it is to be hoped that sand, sebakh, and ruins of houses and tombs still contain many important texts that await discovery. We possess both complete and fragmentary rolls and codices containing literary works or documents; originating from every century of the Greco-Roman period, they are unique testimonies to Egypt's cultural history and mark the mid-point of the book's development, a continual process starting in the third millennium B.C. and carrying on through the Arab-Islamic period right up to our days, irrespective of changes in material, outer form and language.

Roll and Codex

By the middle of the 7th century B.C. at the latest, the papyrus roll was in use in Greece, too. Although no written evidence of this early period has been discovered, it seems obvious that the great epic poems which were written from the 6th century onwards, the lyrics both as solo songs and for choir, the epinician odes of Pindar, tragedies and comedies as well as prose dealing with history and philosophy must have existed in a number of copies. Even if much of the poetry and narrative literature was still recited and passed on orally, written literature spread to an increasing extent and in the second half of the 5th

century B.C. we learn from Greek comedies that bookshops and the book trade connected with them existed in Athens. When at the beginning of the 4th century B.C. Xenophon reports in his "Anabasis" that many written books were found in the wrecks of stranded ships near Salmydessos, it can be assumed that books were also traded overseas. It is certain that Greek books and writing gained immense importance in the century of Plato, Aristotle, Demosthenes and Isocrates; Aristotle's library indicates quite clearly how extensive and valuable even private collections were in some cases.

Until recently our knowledge of the book in Greece was only derived from information provided by their authors, but in 1962 the first papyrus roll was found on Greek soil. During excavations in the village of Dervini, to the north of Salonika, a partly burnt and partly carbonized roll with the text of a commentary on the Orphic theogony was discovered. The writing on this fragment looks very ancient and could justifiably be assigned to the middle of the 4th century B.C. Up to the present the papyrus found at Dervini offers the oldest example of Greek handwriting preserved in the Greek peninsula. Due to the damaged condition of the papyrus the text can only be partially deciphered and a complete restoration of the roll is probably impossible.

The famous Timotheus roll to be found in the Berlin papyrus collection is in a much better state of preservation. Less ancient than the book fragments from Greece, it can be dated with certainty to the last third of the 4th century B.C., perhaps even to the time before Alexander the Great conquered Egypt. This papyrus was found in 1902 near Abu Sir, in the neighbourhood of Cairo, in a tomb where it lay rolled next to the mummy of a man. All the tomb furnishings point to the 4th century, and compared with the oldest dated Greek document—the marriage contract from Elephantine of 311/10 B.C.—the handwriting is cruder. This text is that of a solo sung to the cithara—"The Persians" by Timotheus who wrote this famous work for a festival in about 400 B.C. Apparently the text was incomplete when it was placed in the tomb, because only the last five columns of writing—approximately half the poem—were found. The roll is an example of good craftsmanship. Its sheets are about 19 cms long and 22 cms wide and they have been carefully glued together. The columns of writing consist of about 27 lines each, leaving only a small margin at the head and foot. The length of the lines is uneven, as in many other early literary papyri. The writing shows a skilful hand, but the scribe, who did not keep to the metrical composition of the poetry in dividing his lines, made no attempt to achieve a regular pattern in writing as became the rule in the 3rd century B.C. The Dervini roll and the Timotheus papyrus are not only examples of 4th century B.C. books, they also show the development of the book roll that was largely influenced by Alexandria and stimulated by its famous libraries.

When after the death of Alexander the Great his realm disintegrated as his commanders struggled for the succession, the Macedonian Ptolemy, who was first appointed satrap, taking the royal title in 305 B.C., pursued a sagacious and successful policy so that Egypt became the strongest state militarily and economically of the Eastern Mediterranean. Within the country he relied entirely upon Macedonians and Greeks for his army of mercenaries and for administrators. His successors Ptolemy II and III opened the country on the Nile to these settlers and other newcomers from Asia Minor. What made the first Ptolemies such outstanding rulers was not just the establishment of their position in the country and as a political factor in the Greek world, not just because they strengthened the economy and expanded trade (which also led to the increased export of papyrus rolls), but above all because they made Alexandria a leading Greek intellectual centre. Ptolemy I founded libraries, the museum and Serapeum, but it was only under his son, Ptolemy II Philadelphus, that the city in the western delta gained the position in literature and science it was to hold for centuries. Scholars and poets went to Alexandria to pursue their studies in tranquillity and free from material difficulties; its great research institute had a semi-religious character, with a president-priest heading the Museion, the temple of the muses.

The libraries were the pivot around which all this scholarship revolved. The main one was in the precincts of the king's palace, a subsidiary one being established in the Egyptian suburb of Rhacotis in the temple of Sarapis. They were stocked by buying and copying all available Greek literary works and in the end the subsidiary library had 42,800 and the main one 490,000 rolls. They included the celebrated state edition of tragedies by Aeschylus, Sophocles and Euripides which Ptolemy III had brought from Athens to Alexandria to be copied against a high deposit that he forfeited, keeping the originals. Athens had to content itself with a copy. Distinguished scholars and writers were heads of the library, perhaps the most famous being Callimachus, who devoted himself to catalogues. His most famous work in this field was the "Pinakes" (Tablets), an elaborate compilation of the Alexandrian library listing the literary genre, authors and works, and citing the first words and the number of lines. This general bibliography provided a comprehensive survey of the library's book rolls and laid the foundations for the philological studies which began soon after. We owe the standard texts of Homer, of lyrical and dramatic poetry and of important prose works as well as a wealth of commentaries to this catalogue. Mathematics and natural sciences were also pursued with enthusiasm and again and again during the following centuries outstanding figures emerged in these fields. It can be taken for granted that the libraries needed a large number of scribes in order to extend the stock and replace damaged copies. It was perhaps through these common activities and training that a standard form was established for the writing and layout of the rolls. These rules were not only valid for libraries but for all Greek books in Egypt and beyond its frontiers as long as books were written and read in the form of rolls.

The problems of organizing libraries also certainly influenced the introduction of a standard form of roll. Huge rolls were cumbersome and more liable to damage. That is why a length of about 7 to 10 metres, which could accommodate a Plato dialogue, an official oration by Isocrates or a historical work, was preferred. These standardized rolls almost automatically led to the division of long literary works into chapters and volumes not originally envisaged by the author. The so-called mixed rolls probably contained several short texts. In general the length of the roll corresponded to the length of the work, apart from certain deviations determined by time and taste. Finds confirm that until Byzantine times single sheets were also used for shorter literary texts.

The format of a roll is not only determined by the number of sheets it contains, but also by their height. Although rolls containing records are made up of sheets of varying height because each document was added after its receipt, irrespective of size, the book roll obviously had to be the same height from beginning to end. There was no standard format, and extant rolls range from almost 40 cms down to barely 5 cms. Judging by fragments that have survived, 20 to 30 cms seems to have been the most common format, although small rolls, measuring between 12 and 15 cms in height, were apparently popular among bibliophiles. It is obvious that the height of the sheet also determined the length of the columns of writing. Although it was customary to leave an ample margin at the head and foot because this part of the roll was most subjected to wear and tear, examples of splendid and more especially large-size books show that the columns only occupied two thirds of the sheet. The number of lines, which also depended upon the length of the sheet, varied and was not identical in each column. Short lines, regularly spaced, were regarded as elegant and are often encountered in carefully written rolls. The length of the lines was not dependent on sheet width, but was restricted for the sake of clarity and to facilitate reading. Although in poetry the epic hexameter, the iambic trimeter or senarius in which the dialogue of plays was written, were considered normal lines, in prose works lines consisting of 20 to 30 letters often occurred. Here, too, the attempt was made to keep the lines to the same length and sometimes small pointed hooks were used to fill the line in the right-hand margin, whereas in poetry, due to the varying number of feet, this regularity was not possible at the end of the line.

The books of classical antiquity—whether in the form of a roll or a codex—were usually written in a specially clear and fine book hand, so named to distinguish it from the workaday writing for documents and letters. It is clear that behind both kinds of writing lies an unvarying basic alphabetic form taught in the schools, and skilful scribes used both, according to the content and purpose of a manuscript. But official writing underwent a distinct transformation in the course of the centuries, with special features emerging, and these enable paleographers to approximately date texts according to the writing style, whereas the book hand adhered more strictly to convention. It is thus less easy to recognize its development and to assign it to a particular period. Literary works were written in the scriptura continua, the letters not being grouped into separate words. This involved difficulties for the reader and was abandoned in documents in many cases in favour of word division.

The size of the letters depended probably not only on the taste of the scribe, but also on the current prevailing style; it was certainly influenced by the purpose of the copy and the wishes of whoever ordered it. Although the book hand in general shows a tendency to roundness, ornamental serifs are found on some letters and there is a contrast between the size of long and narrow letters. Generous spacing between lines was always an attractive feature of this book hand. The quality of the writing varied widely and rates of payment differed, too. In his edict of 301 A.D. fixing prices and wages, the Roman Emperor Diocletian laid down maximum prices for a hundred lines of text written in a documentary hand and for first and second class book hand. Although his regulations did not specify any length for a line, the hexa-

meter was probably regarded as normal. Often, but by no means in the majority of cases, the lines are counted, especially in Homer papyri. This helped the scribe to calculate the space necessary for his text; it enabled the library director or the editor to check the copies and calculate the fee and it also provided a guarantee for purchasers that the book was complete. As in the edict, a hundred lines was the standard unit, which was consecutively numbered with letters of the Greek alphabet: alpha, beta, gamma, etc. The citation of numbered lines or verses according to modern literary usage was not customary, so that the occasional numbering of columns was actually superfluous. It was only in legal and administrative practice that records were classified according to tomos (volume) and kollema (number of glued sheets).

It is a fundamental element of literary style that all words should be fully written out, but from the days of the early Roman Empire it was usual to use abbreviations in book rolls, in the same way as had become customary in documents since the 3rd century B.C. Whereas at first the Greek ending "nu" at the end of a line was indicated by a dash above the last letter or a hook on the last vowel, it soon became a regular practice to abbreviate whole and frequently reiterated words, nouns, prepositions or the copula "and" according to set rules. The Berlin papyri collection contains manuscripts like the "Didymus Commentary" or the "Elementary Doctrine of Hierocles" in which such abbreviations are constantly used. Later on there were established contractions for nomina sacra (the names and descriptions of the Trinity and certain derivatives).

A number of signs and accents appeared in literary manuscripts written since the first century B.C. They served to indicate new sentences and paragraphs and the correct pronunciation and stress of words. During the Roman Empire they are found often, especially in Homer, who was frequently read in the schools, and also in older epic, lyric or dramatic texts; but in later books, approximately from the 4th century A.D., they are seldom found. These signs were never used consistently and probably no attempt was made to do so. Weak syllables were marked with a grave accent and strong syllables were circumflexed above the vowel or marked with an acute accent. Spirants were often indicated by the spiritus asper for strong sounds, but the use of the spiritus lenis for weak sounds was less common. Compound words were indicated by a semi-circle underneath the word and proper names often had accents to avoid confusion.

Dots on the line, slightly above it or the high dot separated sentences and paragraphs, and the colon, originally indicating the end of a sentence, was used later on in direct speech to indicate that another person was speaking when this occurred within a line. The paragraphos is very ancient—it is a horizontal dash underneath the beginning of a line in which a sentence or a paragraph ends. In drama and sometimes in prose containing dialogue this dash was used to indicate the change of speaker; extant texts of this kind rarely indicate the various roles by using abbreviations denoting the individual character or chorus. Quotations were either indented or set out or they were marked with pointed hooks at the beginning of the line. Finally the end of longer paragraphs was marked by the coronis, which was sometimes an ornamented paragraphos.

Copies were hardly ever produced without mistakes—the majority of texts show signs of correction—and in principle it does not matter whether the scribe himself corrected his work or left it to somebody else. The corrector frequently added accents, punctuation marks, missing letters or words, or wrote whole verses in the upper or lower margin of a column. Wrong letters were either crossed out or marked with dots; very often both was done. Cases in which the corrector changed the text or the spelling—like substituting the Attic double Tau by the usual double Sigma—are less frequent.

Sometimes it even happened that the corrector overlooked errors or was mistaken in his indications. In general, the number of corrections tended to increase the value of the manuscript.

Many literary papyri contain annotations of different length made perhaps by the corrector, but often also by the reader. Such explanatory additions above the line or in the margin are called scholia; they were intended to make the text understandable and often consist of passages from the many commentaries by Alexandrine grammarians, of which the Berlin Didymus commentary on the speeches of Demosthenes is the most important example. There are also factual explanations, text variations, annotations concerning points of grammar and verse metre as well as a multitude of signs inserted by the critic. The star (asterisk) marks the reiteration of the same words in a text, the pointed obelus indicates that a passage is spurious and the diple, a dash split to the right, a grammatical particularity. Most of the literary texts were of course copied for the extensive book trade and were void of all scholarly notes which were only of value to the educated who could appreciate the finer points of grammar and philology.

It is a matter of uncertainty whether the Greek book roll originally had a title in our sense. The poet Timotheus signed his "Persians" on the last page, but on the well preserved copy no title is mentioned, and the library catalogue of Callimachus does not list titles but the first words of the works, similar to the papal encyclicals of our day. Our roll fragments show that the main title was mentioned in full or in an abridged form at the end of the book, whilst the beginning only had a brief title, an arrangement which we also find in very early codices. Libraries and larger book collections need well-displayed titles for easy reference. These titles were indicated on parchment slips projecting from the rolls. Called "index" or "titulus" in Latin, they were red or yellow and mentioned the author's name and the title of the book. A slat with bent ends, sometimes coloured and ornamented with golden knobs, helped to facilitate the unrolling of the book. But since these slats were not glued on to the papyrus they have disappeared.

For external protection the edges of the book roll (usually only the recto was written on) were sometimes reinforced with strips; a parchment cover which was mostly purple gave added protection. Academic works were no doubt frequently illustrated, for instance with mathematical diagrams drawn with the aid of a ruler, as in the case of the commentary on Plato's "Theaetetus". Mention is also made of portraits of poets contained in books, but only a few illustrations of this kind have survived; some drawings and fragments of coloured sheets used as patterns for weaving and embroidery are still extant. There is evidence that the Greek book roll was used for nearly a thousand years in Egypt and that single copies were still being written when the codex had already become the dominating book form and Egypt had long been conquered by the Arabs; an example is the Easter Epistle by the Patriarch of Alexandria written at the beginning of the 8th century.

It was not on rolls, but in codices that the literature of antiquity spread over Europe in the Middle Ages. When we refer to books nowadays, we naturally mean a codex, which since the Arab conquests was pre-eminent in the Islamic world, too. The beginnings of the codex are perhaps to be found in the loosely bound wooden and waxen tablets which were, however, not easy to handle and formed an unwieldy block when it came to writing longer texts. When instead of wooden tablets, papyrus or parchment sheets that could be folded one inside the other were used, it proved a handy form of writing material for brief notes with the added advantage that both sides of the sheets could be used.

We do not know exactly when the codex as we know it first appeared, but in any case parchment, not papyrus, was used for the new form of book. It seems certain that in the later decades of the Roman Republic senate documents and perhaps also legal reference books existed in the form of codices; through the Roman writer Martial we know that well-known literary works were on sale from the 1st century A.D. in the form of small and apparently cheap parchment codices. Legal literature was probably also copied onto this new kind of book, because it facilitated reference work and eliminated cumbersome rolling. In spite of this, for a long time the codex was considered of less value than the precious book roll, which continued to dominate until the 4th century A.D.

Among the fragments of Greek literature preserved in Egypt's dry soil there are many codex sheets which supply general information about how this new kind of book spread and developed. Although parchment sheets were used first of all, perhaps at the end of the 2nd *71* century, it can be noted that especially in Egypt papyrus soon became the writing material for the new kind of books. Early Christian texts, in particular, used the codex form. We may thus assume that both the Old and the New Testament were known to Christian communities at first in the form of codices, although other texts, like the well-known collection of "Sayings of Jesus", are also extant in roll form. Coptic manuscripts of the early Church, together with those of Gnosticism and Manichaeism have only come to light as codices. But Greek poetry and prose were transcribed more and more on to the new type of book. Thus "Dyscolus", a comedy by *72* Menander, was found in a 3rd century codex which after the Second World War was acquired by the Geneva Bodmer Library and published in 1958. From the 4th century onwards the new book form was generally used, although it did not entirely supersede the roll until a later date.

The putting together of a codex is completely different from that of a roll which always remained a single writing strip. A codex was made by putting single sheets, cut to the same size, on top of each other, stitching them together in the middle and then folding them. Since papyrus in particular was likely to tear round the stitches, a parchment strip was put on the inner sheet. For a long time a codex consisted of a single quire; it was often unwieldy and the inner sheets were narrower so that there was less writing space on them. This continued to be the case even later when several thin quires of 2 to 9 sheets each were used. Although parchment was a more durable material for codices, papyrus was still predominant for many centuries.

Papyrus fragment of a book of weaving patterns, Berlin

However, the three great early Greek codices of the Bible, dating from the 4th and 5th centuries—the Codex Sinaiticus, Codex Alexandrinus and the Codex Vaticanus—are vellum books. The Codex Sinaiticus, discovered by Tischendorf in St. Catharine's Monastery at the foot of Mt. Sinai—after which it was named—consisted of about 730 sheets of which, however, only 390 have survived. The majority of them are in the British Museum and *73* the remainder in the University Library of Leipzig. The Codex Alexandrinus contains the most complete biblical text and is also one of the treasured possessions of the British Museum. It consists of 773 vellum sheets and every page has two columns of writing. Athanasius II presented the Codex to the library of the Alexandrine Patriarch.

There were considerable differences in the format of the codices, just as there were in the rolls. There is nothing particularly remarkable about this fact; the appearance of our books, too, is subject to taste and fashion. Important for the classification of certain groups is the relation of length to width. Up to the 4th century a *71* small format, where the length was almost equal to the width, seems to have prevailed. There are other books, however, in which the length is nearly double the width. The format is not always an indication of the date of origin of the codex. But in general it can be stated that in very early times small sizes predominated and it was only from the 5th century onwards that the large codex *74* became more widespread.

As in the case of the rolls, the amount of writing on a page determined the general impression. Both in rolls and codices it was considered a particularly elegant arrangement to have a narrow column of writing with wide margins around it. It was customary to set lines not exactly in the middle of the page, but closer to the folding line, because outer margins, especially if papyrus was used, suffered the most wear and tear. Most of the codices have only one column on each page, but there are also Greek and Coptic books, especially the great 4th and 5th century *73* codices of the Bible, with several narrow columns on each page. The fine effect produced by these neighbouring columns of writing was probably the reason for adopting this procedure, although the traditional way of writing on the rolls continued to exercise a strong influence. It was not easy to adapt the writing methods used on the rolls to the codices, because the latter's pages were more limited in size, demanding a regular length of line. Although this regularity was not difficult to achieve in prose works, it was more difficult in poetry where the lines varied in length. On most codex fragments the writing itself is extremely even and clear, with rounded, stylized letters very different to the business hand of the time. Accents and punctuation marks are used in the same way as on the rolls, but occur much less frequently after the 4th century. The division of paragraphs follows traditional practice. In Christian texts, sentences are sometimes numbered and a division into verses can be observed. And the larger and frequently coloured initials, set out a little to the left at the introduction of a new subject, were soon in general use. A new feature was the numbering of pages which, however, only developed gradually. Despite the obvious advantages of numbering the pages of a codex, especially where a work of reference was concerned, this was not always done. Sometimes only every second page was numbered and sometimes only the quires.

It might be assumed that the book in its new form, with its first page protected by a cover, would have resulted in putting the title of the work at the beginning, where it belongs, but in this respect, too, the roll maintained its influence for a long time. Early codices had an abbreviated title at the beginning and the main title was put at the end, as for instance in the Codex Sinaiticus and Codex Alexandrinus. It was only slowly and probably as a result of the growing tendency to add the names of the scribe, the corrector or the editor to the title at the end of the book that the main title was transferred to the beginning. The title at the end was thus replaced by a subscript. This development probably came to an end about 400 A.D.

The habit of dividing and stressing parts of the texts through the use of subtitles was also maintained. The numbering of verses and lines in works of poetry and prose became common practice in the course of time and the number of lines is often indicated at the end of a paragraph.

Examples of book illustrations are only extant since the Byzantine period, mainly in Bible manuscripts, although according to literary quotations they were already known at the time of the Roman Empire. These drawings and coloured paintings apparently met a widespread wish to have uniform texts illustrated and explained by pictures. Illustrations were soon combined with decorative elements, especially at the end of a book, and from the 4th century, Greek and Coptic texts display larger and often coloured and ornamented initial letters set out a little to the left.

Book-bindings consisted very often of papyrus sheets which were glued together and mostly strengthened with ornamented leather covers. Only a few examples have survived from the centuries of Roman rule; most of them are Coptic codices.

It seems certain that the books were not written after they had been made up into codices but on separate quires; codices consisting of only one quire were written on single sheets placed one on top of the other. Nevertheless, there must have been cases where the writing was done after the book had been stitched together. Sometimes scribes miscalculated the space available for their texts and as a result the writing on the last page is either very cramped or—in a minority of cases—very widely spaced. The numbering of pages and quires was undertaken not only for the benefit of the reader, but more often to help the scribe to copy his material in the right order. If major corrections had to be made or parts of the text were missing, it was possible to replace the pages concerned by single sheets. Despite the individual style of some of the scribes, the book hand of the codices, especially those of the 4th and 5th centuries, has a fine regularity in its lettering and arrangement of columns. The lines are often indicated by dots on the left and drawn with the aid of a ruler. This regularity is maintained in Coptic manuscripts until well into the Arab period.

Captions to the Illustrations

51 *Ink drawing on papyrus.* On the recto of a papyrus sheet, whose verso contains an account dating from Arab times, Dionysus is pictured together with a panther on the left behind him with its head pointing towards the god. Dionysus stands naked in the foreground with his right arm raised, holding the thyrsus in his left. This modest drawing in the Greek style was perhaps an illustration to one of the numerous Dionysus works that retained their popularity well into the late Roman Empire—Nonnos' "Dionysiaca" for example.

Staatliche Museen zu Berlin, Papyrus-Sammlung, P 9927. Papyrus; 13.5 × 12.5 cms. Egypt, origin unknown; about 5th—7th century A.D.

52 *Papyrus fragment of a book of weaving patterns.* The coloured pattern shows decorative plants with blossoms, intermingled with birds and animals, and swans in the medallions. The whole pattern is circular and enclosed in a decorative square. Staatliche Museen zu Berlin, Papyrus-

Sammlung, P 9926. Papyrus; 17×7.5 cms. Egypt, origin unknown; 4th—6th century A.D. W. Schubart, Miniaturen auf Papyrus, Amtliche Berichte aus den königlichen Kunstsammlungen, XXX, Berlin 1908, Sp. 294 and following; P. W. Scheller, A Survey of Medieval Model Books, Haarlem 1963, page 46, Cat. No. 2

59 *Document from the chancellery of the Roman governor of Egypt.* The hand of four different scribes can be distinguished in this original document written in the chancellery of the Roman Prefect Subatianus Aquila. Beneath the carefully written large letters of the business hand are the personal signature of the governor with the conventional form of address, a note to the effect that the document had been scrutinized by the scribe's superior and the date. The letter addressed to Theon, the military commander of the province of Arsinoe (Fayyum) orders the release of a prisoner sentenced to five years' labour in the stone quarries. The narrow parchment strip on the left of the document has also survived. Staatliche Museen zu Berlin, Papyrus-Sammlung, P 11532. Papyrus; 22×32 cms. Presumably from Theadelphia (Fayyum); 209 A.D. F. Zucker, Urkunde aus der Kanzlei eines römischen Statthalters von Ägypten in Originalausfertigung, Sitz. Ber. d. Preuss. Akad. d. Wiss., phil.-hist. Kl., XXXVII (1910), Berlin, page 710 and following; G. Cavallo, La scrittura del P. Berol. 11532 contributo allo studio dello stile di cancelleria nei papiri breci di età romana, Aegyptus XLV (1965), page 216 and following

59 *Fragment of a papyrus roll in Latin containing the speech of a Roman emperor.* Of the few Latin texts found in Egypt this speech of a Roman emperor, possibly Claudius (41—54 A.D.), is specially valuable. Only three columns are extant; they indicate that the Emperor in a speech to the Senate dealt with questions of criminal procedure. Staatliche Museen zu Berlin, Papyrus-Sammlung, P 8507. Papyrus; 28.5×65 cms. Egypt, origin unknown; 1st century A.D. Published by O. Gradenwitz and F. Krebs BGU II (1898) No. 611; R. Cavenaile, Corpus Papyrorum Latinarum, 4. Lief., Wiesbaden 1958, No. 236.

60 *Hieratic papyrus with the text of the Book on Breathing.* Among the funerary papyri that were intended to help the dead on their passage through the underworld and to face the ordeal of judgement was the "Book on Breathing". The reproduction shows the first column of the hieratic illustrated papyrus roll which dates from the early Roman Empire. Staatliche Museen zu Berlin, Papyrus-Sammlung, P 3135. Papyrus; 26×164 cms. Possibly from Thebes; 2nd or 3rd century A.D. G. Möller, Hieratische Paläographie, Vol. 3, Leipzig 1936, page 15 and Plate XI; also by the same author, Hieratische Lesestücke für den akademischen Gebrauch, No. 3, Berlin 1961 (reprint), page 32

61 *Demotic papyrus document.* The contract, consisting of a few very long lines, documents an agreement between two brothers to sell their share in a tomb. Beneath the demotic text is the receipt (written in Greek) of the royal bank of Thebes for the duty payable on conclusion of a sale. The reproduction depicts a section with the beginning of the document written from right to left. Staatliche Museen zu Berlin, Papyrus-Sammlung, P 3119. Papyrus; 30×116 cms. Thebes; 146 B.C. W. Spiegelberg, Demotischer Papyrus aus den Königl. Museen zu Berlin, Leipzig-Berlin 1902, p. 10 and following and Plates 17/18; the receipt in Greek is taken from U. Wilcken, Urkunden der Ptolemäerzeit, Vol. II, 2. Lief., Berlin-Leipzig 1937, No. 175 b

61 *Greek translation of a demotic contract of sale.* The document consists of two columns; the first, partially destroyed, is an application to the administration and the second the complete text of a Greek translation of a demotic contract of sale. There was obviously disagreement between the two parties about the part of the estate to be sold. Staatliche Museen zu Berlin, Papyrus-Sammlung P 9795. Papyrus; 23.5×70 cms. Hermopolis; 55 B.C. Published by W. Schubart, BGU III (1898—1903) No. 1002

62 *Greek document from the Royal Theban Bank.* The letter written by Dionysius, the deputy thebarch, to the head of the bank of the province of Diogenes belongs, together with two other documents, to the records of the Theban royal bank. It concerns the remarkable story of 150 copper talents that the priests of Amonrasonther ("Amon-Re, king of the gods", who was worshipped at Karnak as the main Theban deity) had paid to the bank for the appointment of a temple scribe. Dionysius employed the money for other purposes and subsequently attempted to put matters right by demanding the return of certain documents and paying back the sum out of his own pocket. Staatliche Museen zu Berlin, Papyrus-Sammlung, P 1389 Verso. Papyrus; 31×18 cms. Thebes; 131 B.C. Published by U. Wilcken, Urkunden der Ptolemäerzeit, Vol. II, 3. Lief., Berlin 1957, No. 199

62 *Official letter written by the military commander Dionysius to the royal scribe Paniskus.* In the letter written by Dionysius, the military commander of the province of Heracleopolis to his deputy, the royal scribe Paniskus, an order is given for the transport of 1,200 measures of corn by river to Alexandria. From the added copy of the bill of consignment, a column is missing on the right. The document came to light among the papyri wrappings at Abu Sir el-meleq. Staatliche Museen zu Berlin, Papyrus-Sammlung, P 13952. Papyrus; 32.5×30.3 cms. Province of Heracleopolis; 64/63 B.C. Published by W. Kunkel, Verwaltungsakten aus spätptolemäischer Zeit, APF VIII (1927), page 187; BGU VIII (1933), No. 1741

62 *Aramaic papyrus with a petition to the Persian satrap Bagoas.* The Jewish community of the military colony on Elephantine possessed a temple of their god Jehovah which was destroyed in 410 B.C. by the Egyptians assisted by Persian soldiers. As the satrap of Egypt was absent, the community sent a petition, written in Aramaic, to Bagoas, the satrap of Judaea, in 407 B.C. It contained the request to rebuild the temple which, according to the cult reform decreed by Esra and Nehemiah, would have been a forbidden act. Another document indicates that this request was granted. The reproduction depicts the recto of the letter. Staatliche Museen zu Berlin, Papyrus-Sammlung, P 13595. Papyrus; 24.5×32 cms. Elephantine; 407 B.C. Published by E. Sachau, Aramäische Papyrus und Ostraka aus einer jüdischen Militär-Kolonie zu Elephantine, Leipzig 1911, Pap. I; B. Porten, Archives from Elephantine, University of California Press, Berkeley and Los Angeles 1968

63 *Papyrus sheet with two copies of a Greek marriage contract.* The marriage contract of 311/10 B.C., which in 1906 was found folded and sealed in an earthenware jar together with other early Ptolemaic papyri in a ruin on Elephantine, is the oldest dated Greek document from Egypt and thus the oldest Greek original contract in existence. The text of the document is written twice; both copies were folded and rolled; the upper copy (the inside one) being sealed while the lower copy (the outside one) could be read at any time. Six Greeks are named at the end of the document as witnesses to the marriage contract of Herakleides and Demetria from Kos; they were all members of the military colony on Elephantine, the main garrison in southern Egypt. Staatliche Museen zu Berlin, Papyrus-Sammlung, P 13500. Papyrus; 40×35 cms. Elephantine; 2 311/10 B.C. Published by O. Rubensohn, Elephantine-Papyri, Berlin 1907, No. I

63 *Sealed Greek documents.* The three sealed documents, like the marriage contract, are numbered among the oldest dated Greek original documents from Egypt. The seals and signatures of the witnesses to the contracts can be seen on these reproductions. Staatliche Museen zu Berlin, Papyrus-Sammlung, P 13503, P 13504, P 13501, Papyrus. Elephantine; 385–383 B.C. Published by O. Rubensohn, Elephantine-Papyri, Plate 1; Texts Nos. IV, III and II

64 *Papyrus roll with passages from the Gnomon of the Idios Logos.* This copy of passages from the Gnomon of the Idios Logos contains more than a hundred various edicts of Roman law and of the provincial government of Egypt as far as they concerned the special financial authority that administered Egyptian cult affairs, too. This collection of edicts issued by the Emperor Augustus, the Senate, the respective governors and authorities of the Idios Logos is a legal document of the first importance from the time of the early Roman Empire. This copy, which was made about 150 A.D., is written on the back of a report made by the granary storekeeper of the village of Bernikis Aigialu (Fayyum) about the daily tax payments in kind and covers a period of 3 months during 149 A.D. The reproduction is of the conclusion of the text with the final numbered edicts. Staatliche Museen zu Berlin, Papyrus-Sammlung, P 11650. Papyrus; 21×209 cms. Theadelphia (Fayyum); about 150 A.D. Published by W. Schubart, BGU V,1 (1919); W. Graf Uxkull-Gyllenband, BGU V,2 (1934); S. Riccobono jr., Il Gnomon dell' Idios Logos, Palumbo 1950; recto; H. Kortenbeutel, BGU IX (1937), No. 1893

65 *Papyrus sheet with an instruction to Zenon and the copy of a letter written by Apollonius.* A tenant farmer of the Finance Minister Apollonius was arrested, presumably because he had not paid his salt tax. Zenon is requested to see that the peasant is released so that his land may be irrigated. In the accompanying dated copy of a letter written by Apollonius the latter forbids the tax collectors to press the peasants of the village of Tapteia to pay their salt tax. Egyptian Museum, Cairo, L 8578, 59130 (Catalogue Général), 830–48578. Papyrus; 31×8.5 cms. Philadelphia (Fayyum); 255 B.C. Published by C. C. Edgar, P. Cairo Zenon I (Zenon-Papyri), Cairo 1925, No. 59130

65 *Papyrus sheet with a list of Zenon's attire.* This list of articles of clothing belonging to Zenon, which were obviously needed for his extensive journeys accompanying Apollonius, the Finance Minister, contains both summer and winter wear, including 11 chitons and six coats (chlamys). Egyptian Museum, Cairo, L. 8540, 59092 (Catalogue Général), 793–48540 Papyrus; 33.5×18.5 cms. Philadelphia (Fayyum); middle of the 3rd century B.C. Published by C. C. Edgar, P. Cairo Zenon I (Zenon-Papyri), Cairo 1925, No. 59092; for general information: C. Préaus, Les Grecs en Egypte d'après les archives de Zénon, Brussels 1947

66 *Papyrus roll of "The Persians" by Timotheus (Col. V).* The illustration depicts the conclusion of the account of the Battle of Salamis (480 B.C.); at line 14 begins the sphragis, the last part of the nomos, in which the poet expresses his views. The stiff, antiquated writing is divided into lines of irregular length. The description and sphragis are separated by the paragraphos and coronis in the form of a bird on the left margin. Staatliche Museen zu Berlin, Papyrus-Sammlung, P 9875. Papyrus; as from Col. II 115×91 cms. Abu Sir; last part of the 4th century B.C. Published by U. v. Wilamowitz-Moellendorf, Timotheos, Die Perser, Leipzig 1903; Pack, No. 1537

67 *Greek mathematical ostracon.* This earthen fragment, broken off at the top, right and bottom, contains the oldest Greek mathematical text found in Egypt. With reference to

Euclid, it gives the solution and demonstration of the problem of how to draw a regular icosahedron in a sphere with a given diameter. This was at that time one of the most complicated problems of pure mathematics. Staatliche Museen zu Berlin, Papyrus-Sammlung, P 12609. Potsherd; 10.5×9 cms. Elephantine; about the middle of the 3rd century B.C. Published by J. Mau and W. Müller, Mathematische Ostraka aus der Berliner Sammlung, APF Vol. 17 (1960/62) page 1 and following; Pack, No. 2323

67 *Sheet of papyrus with Greek drinking songs and an elegy.* The sheet served as a cover for sealed documents (Ill. 65), the oldest of which dates back to the early part of the 3rd century B.C. The verses could belong to the same period for they are evocative of the soldier's life as experienced by the Macedonian and Greek troops stationed on Elephantine. The elegy at the end of the text is actually the introduction to the feast itself. In the left-hand margin of this papyrus fragment three songs are noted in writing that slopes upwards. It was probably a private copy of the drinking songs which were sung as solos with flute accompaniment. Staatliche Museen zu Berlin, Papyrus-Sammlung, P 13270. Papyrus; 24.5×33 cms. Elephantine; about the 3rd century B.C. Published by W. Schubart and U. v. Wilamowitz-Moellendorff, BKT V,2 Berlin 1907, No. XV; Pack, No. 1924

68 *Greek papyrus with notes of music.* On the verso of a Latin military invoice dating from 156 A.D. is a column torn off on the right, from a manual of music. Fragments of several Greek poems written in sprawling letters have the customary alphabetic indication of the vocal notes over the line; the instrumentation which was perhaps for a wind instrument (aulos) is indicated separately. Staatliche Museen zu Berlin, Papyrus-Sammlung, P 6870. Papyrus; 35×24 cms. Upper Egypt, Contrapollinopolis (?); about 200 A.D. Published by W. Schubart, Ein griechischer Papyrus mit Noten, Sitz. Ber. d. Preuss. Akad. d. Wiss., phil.-hist. Kl., XXXVI (1918), Berlin, page 763 and following; Pack, No. 2439

68 *Greek tax roll from Theadelphia (Fayyum).* This document roll, which is more than 6 metres in length, contains lists of several categories of taxes. The reproduction depicts one of the columns—the rest is rolled up on the right and left. Staatliche Museen zu Berlin, Papyrus-Sammlung, P 11651. Papyrus; 30×620 cms. Theadelphia (Fayyum); 166 A.D. Published by H. Kortenbeutel, BGU IX (1937) No. 1896, 1897, 1897a

69 *Papyrus roll with parts of the commentary on Plato's "Theaetetus".* This largest papyrus text from commentaries written in antiquity contains 75 columns and several small fragments of an explanatory text to Plato's dialogue "Theaetetus". After being read the papyrus roll was obviously not rolled up again, so that the beginning was found inside when it was opened. The beginning of the text was undoubtedly missing in classical times; about a third of the whole commentary is extant and its author is unknown. Only one side of the roll was used and it was made up of carefully glued sheets. With its regular, narrow columns, clear writing and wide margin at the head and foot it may be considered a particularly fine example of the book trade. The quotations from Plato are indicated by hooks to the left of the text and in two instances (Col. 31 and 43—see illustration) drawings are used to explain the mathematical text. The scribe used hooks to fill his lines, reading signs, abbreviation marks over "nu" at the end of the line, and in some cases accents and tried to divide the words correctly. The corrections done in a cursive hand are not in every case consistent or accurate. Staatliche Museen zu Berlin, Papyrus-Sammlung, P 9782. Papyrus; 30×600 cms. Hermopolis; 2nd century A.D. Published by H. Diels and W. Schubart, Anonymer Kommentar zu Platons Theaetet, BKT II, Berlin 1905; Pack, No. 1393

69 *Papyrus roll with parts of the Didymus commentary on Demosthenes' speeches.* From the multitude of scholarly commentaries on the works of classical Greek literature written by the grammarian Didymus (1st century B.C.), only this roll is extant. It contains the last 15 columns of a commentary on Demosthenes, 9th to 12th speeches attacking Philip II of Macedonia (4th century B.C.). As the conclusion of the work with the title indicates, this is the third roll from a series of 28 commentaries. The four speeches were indicated by their opening words. The text, written in a careless, almost cursive 2nd century A.D. hand, contains many abbreviations and a number of corrections which are not always accurate. It may be concluded that the scribe was not particularly painstaking. The quotations from the speeches discussed are set out on the left; individual sections are indicated by paragraphos and coronis within the columns numbering about 70 lines; they also have separate headings. The inner and outer appearance of the roll indicates that it was probably a private copy, possibly an excerpt. There is a philosophical treatise on the verso of the papyrus: Hierocles' Ethical Elementary Doctrine. Staatliche Museen zu Berlin, Papyrus-Sammlung, P 9780. Papyrus; 30×134 cms. Hermopolis (?); 2nd century A.D. Published by H. Diels and W. Schubart, Didymos, Kommentar zu Demosthenes, BKT I, Berlin 1904; Pack, No. 339. Verso: H. v. Arnim, Hierokles, Ethische Elementarlehre, BKT IV, Berlin 1907, Pack, No. 536

70 *Easter Epistle by the Patriarch of Alexandria (papyrus roll).* The announcement of the celebration of Easter for the Church of Egypt was one of the duties of the Patriarch of Alexandria, and already in early times, the announcement of the date was associated with the preaching of a sermon, for which Athanasius became especially celebrated. This Easter

Epistle (Col. VIII) with its large and handsome writing originates from the chancellery of the Patriarch of Alexandria, presumably from Alexander II, and was sent at the beginning of the 8th century A.D. to Gennathius, thought to be the abbot of the White Monastery near Sohag in Upper Egypt. The scribe has made some corrections in his text; there are very few accents and other reading signs and the spelling is perfectly correct. With reference to the beginning of the Gospel according to St. John, the sermon defends the teachings of the Monophysites and attacks the orthodox dogma that the two natures in Christ, the human and the divine, had remained separate. The roll consists of 20 sheets and contains 11 columns; the Greek-Arabic protocol at the beginning of the roll with the name of the addressee on the verso is extant in fragmentary form. Staatliche Museen zu Berlin, Papyrus-Sammlung, P 10677. Papyrus; 45 × 500 cms. White Monastery near Sohag (Upper Egypt); early 8th century A.D. Published by C. Schmidt and W. Schubart, Altchristliche Texte, BKT VI, Berlin 1910, V

71 *Fragment of a papyrus roll with poetry by Alcaeus.* These few fragments of verse from poems by Alcaeus, who lived on Lesbos at about 600 B.C., are written on two columns of the verso of a sheet of papyrus that was obviously part of a roll. The individual sections are marked by the paragraphos and the end of the poem by the coronis (Col. II). To the left of an indented line of a further poem a scholium (annotation) has been added by the same hand, but in smaller writing. Staatliche Museen zu Berlin, Papyrus-Sammlung, P 9569. Papyrus; 10.5 × 8 cms. Egypt, Fayyum; 1st-2nd century A.D. Published by W. Schubart and U. v. Wilamowitz-Moellendorff, BKT V,2, Berlin 1907, No. XII,1; Pack, No. 60

71 *Page from a parchment codex: "The Cretans" by Euripides.* This fragment from the otherwise unknown drama "The Cretans" by Euripides with indented lyrical chorus passages and a longer speech by Pasiphae, whose name stands to the left of Line 4, comes from a parchment codex of small format, whose extant page is partially destroyed. The text, written in an elegant and regular book hand, includes accents in some places but also contains a number of mistakes. Staatliche Museen zu Berlin, Papyrus-Sammlung, P 13217. Parchment; 14.5 × 10.5 cms. Hermopolis; 2nd century A.D. Published by W. Schubart and U. v. Wilamowitz-Moellendorff, BKT V,2, Berlin 1907, No. XVII,1; Pack, No. 437

71 *Wax tablet book.* The nine wooden tablets covered with wax were bound together with rings or thread drawn through the four openings. They were used for school exercises, e.g. division of syllables, and simple accountancy. It is presumed that the codex, the form of book still in use today, developed out of these bound wax tablets. The writing done on the soft wax with metal styles was easy to erase by smoothing the surface. Staatliche Museen zu Berlin, Papyrus-Sammlung, P 14000. Wax tablets; 17.5 × 9.5 cms. each. Egypt, origin unknown; 4th—5th century A.D. Published by G. Plaumann, Antike Schultafeln aus Ägypten, Amtliche Berichte aus den Königlichen Kunstsammlungen, XXXIV, Berlin 1913, Sp. 210 and following; Pack, No. 2737

72 *Page from a papyrus codex of the comedy "Dyscolus" by Menander.* The first completely preserved comedy by the Attic poet Menander (about 300 B.C.) starts on page 19 of a papyrus codex and its 969 verses in which the chorus parts are omitted fill 11 sheets, i.e. 21 pages. Before the text we find the contents in the form of verses, which name the well-known grammarian Aristophanes of Byzantium (3rd-2nd century B.C.) as their author, the didascalia and the dramatis personae. The reproduction shows the text on page 28, written in a flowing hand that slopes slightly to the right. The names of the characters, sometimes abbreviated, are given on the left. A change of speaker within a verse is generally indicated by a colon and paragraphos and spoken verses from the omitted passages sung by the chorus are in each case indicated by a diple at the beginning and end of the last line. Bibliotheca Bodmeriana, P. Bodmer IV. Papyrus; 27.5 × 13 cms. Upper Egypt, Panopolis (?); 3rd century A.D. Published by V. Martin, Papyrus Bodmer IV, Ménandre; Le Dyscolos, Bibliothèque Bodmer, Cologny-Genève 1958 (private edition); Pack, No. 1298

73 *Vellum page from the Codex Sinaiticus.* The Codex Sinaiticus is considered the oldest of the great Bible codices of classical times. The majority of its sheets are in the British Museum. Each page contains four columns with mostly 48 lines; at a later date the Eusebian commentaries and canons were added in the margin. The regular writing, with the first letter of each new passage set out, was the work of several painstaking scribes. There are many corrections; reading signs and punctuation are missing. The reproduced page is from the New Testament (St. Matt. XXVII, 30—64), British Museum, Cat. No. Mss/91965. Vellum 43 × 37 cms. St. Catherine's Monastery, Sinai, second half of the 4th century A.D.

73 *Page from a parchment codex of the "Iliad".* The extant parchment page belongs to the outer double sheet of a quire consisting of four pages. This fine copy of the "Iliad" is in large, regular writing and includes accents. Page 3 which is reproduced here contains the verses 390—431 of book XXII. Staatliche Museen zu Berlin, Papyrus-Sammlung, 6794. Parchment; 22 × 43.5 cms. Egypt, Fayyum; 4th—5th century A.D. Mentioned in BKT V,1 Berlin 1907, page 3; Pack, No. 984; G. Cavallo, Ricerche sulla maiuscola biblica, Firenze 1967, Plate 80

74 *Page from a papyrus codex with parts of a Latin-Greek-Coptic conversation book*. On a single page of the codex fragments of conversations are arranged in two columns. They are given in Latin, Greek and Coptic. The translated words are generally separated by colons. Whereas the Latin and Greek text is correct on the whole, the Coptic (Sahidic) version has many omissions and mistakes. The writing which shows Coptic influences is, however, Greek in style and in several places badly faded and almost illegible as can be seen from this reproduction of Page 2. Latin was obviously learnt in Egypt through the medium of Latin-Greek conversation books which were then translated into Coptic. Staatliche Museen zu Berlin, Papyrus-Sammlung, P 10582. Papyrus; 26.5 × 19 cms. Egypt, origin unknown; 5th—6th century A.D. Published by W. Schubart, Ein lateinisch-griechisch-koptisches Gesprächsbuch, Klio Vol. XIII (1913), page 27 and following; R. Cavenaile, Corpus Papyrorum Latinarum, Lief. 4, Wiesbaden 1958, No. 281; Pack, No. 3009

59 Document from the chancellery of the Roman governor of Egypt, Berlin
    Fragment of a papyrus roll in Latin containing the speech of
    a Roman emperor, Berlin

60 Hieratic papyrus with the text of the Book on Breathing, Berlin

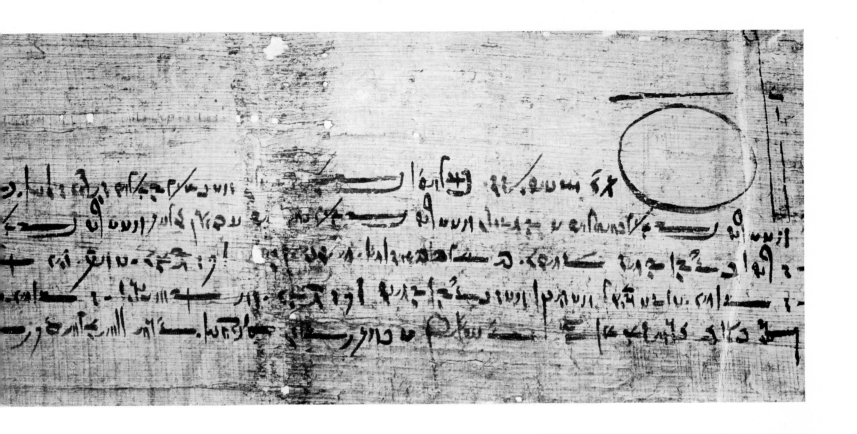

Demotic papyrus document, Berlin
Greek translation of a demotic contract of sale, Berlin

62 Greek document from the Royal Theban
Bank, Berlin
Official letter written by the military
commander Dionysius to the royal scribe
Paniskus, Berlin
Aramaic papyrus with a petition to the
Persian satrap Bagoas, Berlin

63 Papyrus sheet with two copies of a Greek
marriage contract, Berlin
Sealed Greek documents, Berlin

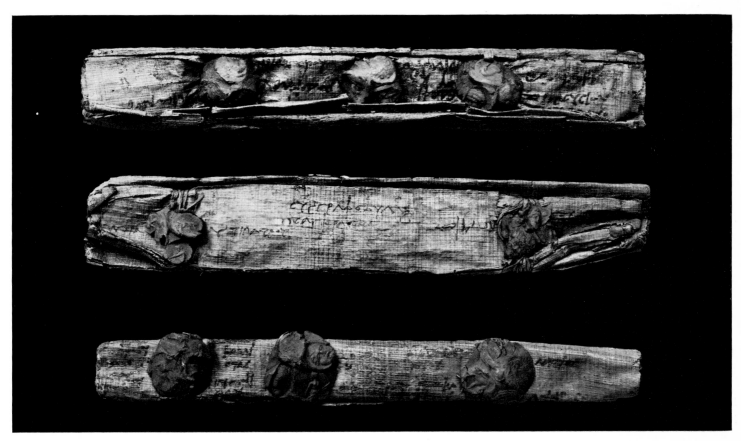

Papyrus roll with passages from the Gnomon of the Idios
Logos, Berlin

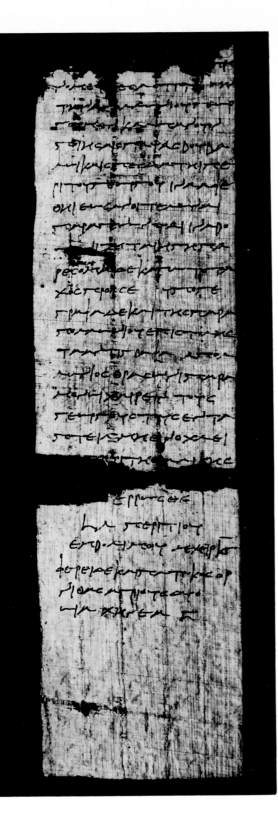

Papyrus sheet with an instruction to Zenon and the copy of a letter written by Apollonius, Cairo
Papyrus sheet with a list of Zenon's attire, Cairo

Papyrus roll of "The Persians" by Timotheus, Berlin

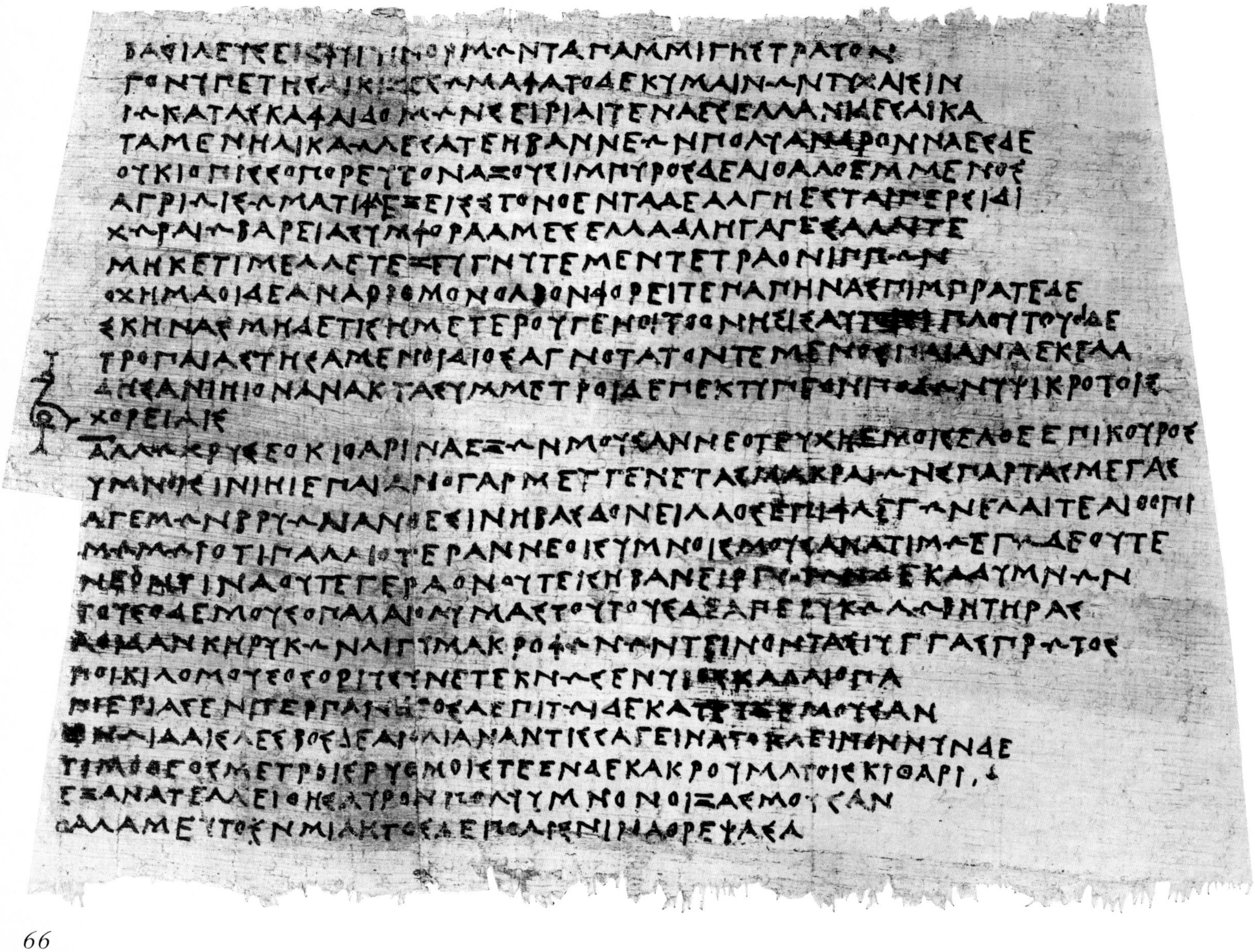

Greek mathematical ostracon, Berlin
Sheet of papyrus with Greek drinking songs and an elegy, Berlin

68 Greek papyrus with notes of music, Berlin
Greek tax roll from Theadelphia (Fayyum), Berlin

69 Papyrus roll with parts of the commentary on Plato's
"Theaetetus", Berlin
Papyrus roll with parts of the Didymus commentary on
Demosthenes' speeches, Berlin

70 Easter Epistle by the Patriarch of Alexandria (papyrus roll), Berlin

71 Fragment of a papyrus roll with poetry by Alcaeus, Berlin
Page from a parchment codex: "The Cretans" by Euripides, Berlin
Wax tablet book, Berlin

ΟΧΛΟϹ ΩϹΕΟ· ΜΝΑϹΕΞΗΜΙΘΟϹΑ
ΦΕΡΘΕ · ΤΙΔϹΤ· ΕΡΗϹΟΝΤΑΙΤΑϹϹΕΠΡΟΙΞΟΝ·
ΑΝΙΔΗΓΑΡΕΝΥ ΝΤΟΝΠΑΝΑΤΕ
ΤΟΝΠΗΟΝΟΙΤΟΥ ΙΔΟΧΟΥΛΕΘΟΞΙΟΙ
ΦΤΟΟΝΤΟϹΕΤΟΥϹ ϳΩΕΩΡΑΚΕΝΕΝΠΑΝΙΟΝ·
ΑΝΘΡΩΠΕΜΜΑΟΙΚΟΠΤΕ·ΟΜΩϹΠΟΝΙΕΤΑ
ΤΙϹΙΘΕΝ·ΗΚΟΚ ΗΜΕΝΗ·ΤΙΠΡΟϹΘΕΩΝ·
ΑΠΟΛΗϹΕΔΟΚΗΤΟΝΠΤΥΝΑ·ΤΟΥΤΟΝΙΕΤΗΟ·
ΤΟΥΤΟΝ·ΑΠΤΟΙΘΝ·ΤΩΤΡΟΦΙΜΩΤΩϹΩϹΤΡΑΤΟϳ·
ΚΟΜΤΩΙΓΝΕΑΝΙϹΚΩϳ·ΠΕΡΙΚΡΟΥΘΠΠΑΓΑϹ·
ΑΠΟΜΟΝ·ΘΤΑΔΟΝΤΑϹΔΑΦΘΘΡΑΝΤΕΚΑϳ
ΔΙΚΕΜΟΝΤΟΠΠΗϹΟΝΤΩΧΩΡΙΩϳ
ϹΚΑΠΤΕΝΚΕΛΕΥΟΝ·ΑΤΟΠΟΝ·ΔΑΛΛΟΥΜΕΝ
ΔΥϹΤΟΥϳΝϹϹΒΘΑΙΟΝΑΠΟΒΥΗΤΟΦΘΒΡΟΝ·
ΚΑΝΑΝΤΑΡ ΜΕΜΔΘΑΚΑϹΤΩΝΝϹΥΡΟΥϹΤΑΝΤΙΚϹΦΕϹ
ΕϳϹΩΠΟΙΗϹΩΜΕΝϹΤΒΘΔΑϹΕΝΔΟΝΕΥΠΡΕΠΗϹ
ΚΑΠΑΛΛΕΤΟϳΜΑΜΗΘϹΕΝΕΠΙΚΩΝΕΤΩ
ΘΤϹΕΙΝ·ΕΠΑΝΕΛΘΟϹΙΝΑΛΛΑΤΛΘΗΠΥΧΛΙ
ΚΡΥΤΑϹΟΦΡΥϹΑΝΕϹΠΟΤϹΤΡΙϹΔΘΝΕ
ΓΕΠϹ ΕΠΩϹΕΧΟΡΤΑϹΩΚΑΤΑϹΤΡΟΠΟΝΤΗϹΗΜΕΡΟΝ·
ΕΠΑΝΕΤΗϹΟΝΗΜϹΟΥΚΑΠΗϹΤΕΧΝΗϹ
ΕΓΩΓΕϹΠΟΤΟΥΧΗϹΤΕΓΩϹΔΟΜΩϹ·

  ΧΟΡΟΥ

ΚΝΗΜΩΝ ΓΡΑΥΤΗΝΘΥΡΑΝ ΚΗϹ ΔϹ ΑΝΟΙΓΕΜΗΔΕΝ
ΕΩϹΑΝΕΛΘΩΔΕΥΡΕΓΩΠΑΛΙΝϹΚΟΤΟΥϹ
ΕϹΤΗΔΕΤΟΧΤΟΠΑΝΤΕΛΩϹΩϹΩϳΜΗ
ϹΤΝϹ ΠΑΛΓΩΝΠΑΡΕΝΟΥΘΑΤΟΝΗΔΗΤΟΥΚΕΝΗ
ΗΜΑϹΕΑϹ·ΤΟΥΠΟΚΑΚΟΝΤϳΒΟΥΤΕΜϳ
ΟΧΛΟϹΤΙϹΑΠΩϹΕϹΚΟΡΑΚΑϹ·ΔΥΝΗΠΟΘΕΝϳ
ΚΝΗΜ
ΠΑΝΟϹΕΩΠΗΦΑϹΠΟΥΤΩϳΠΩΘΕΩϳ
ΟΥϹΗΠΡΟϹΕΝΟϳ·ΝΗΔϳΑΠΕϹΩΘΗΤΕ
ΩΗΡΑΚΛΕϹΛΗΔΑϹΚΛΘΗΜΕΘΟ
ΧΡΟΝΟΝΤΟϹΟΥΤΟΝΠΘΡΙΜΕΝΟΝΤΕϹΥΠΡΘΠΗ
ΑΠΑΝΤΑΔϳΗΜΙΝΕΤΗ·ΝΗΜΑΤΟΝΔϳϳϳ
ΤΟΓΟΥΑΠΡΟΒΑΤΟΝΜΙΚΡΟΥΤΕΘΝΗΚΕΠΡΟϹΛΝΛΝ
ΟΥΠΕΡΙΜΕΝΕΤΗΝϹΑΝΕϹΧΩΝΔΑϹΕΙΤΕ
ΚΑΝΑΠΡΟΧΡΗΔΧΕΝϳΒΔϹΘΥΤΗΜΟΤΙ
ΠΟϳΘΤΕΠΟϳΚΕΧΟΝΔϹ ΘΡΟΝΤΙϹΘΥ·
ΚΝΗΜ ΕΥΚΟϳΧΟΚΙΩϹ ΑΠΟΝΟϳϹΘΠΟϳΟΚΑΝΓΕΛΕ
ΑΡΓΟϳ·ΚΑΤΑϹΤΠΗΓΑΡΜΟΝΗΗΤΗΝΟϳΚΙΩΝ
ΟΥϳ ΑΝΔΥΝΜΜΑΗΝ ΔΙΘΝΙΑϹΦΥΜΗΚΑΚΟΝ
ϳΟΠΤΟϹϳΚΦϹΩϹΤΕΜΟϳΔΟΚΟϹΠΛΛΝ
ΟϳΚΑΔΟΜΗϹΗΝΚΑΤΑΒΑΛΛΩΝΤΗΝΟϳΚΙΑΝ
ϹΘϳΝΙΩϹΟΥΟΥϹΙΔϳΟΠΤΟϳΧΩΡΥΚΟϳ
ΥΦΕΡΟΝΤΥϹΤΑΛΝϳΟΥΧϳΤΩΝΟΘΕΩΝ
ϹΑΛΕϳΠΟΝΟΜΘΒ ΛΝϳΩϹΟϹΕΥϹΕΒΘϹ
ΤΟΠϳΝΟΝΠΟΥΤΘϳΔΘΝΟΘΘϹΘϹΕΠϳΛΠΩΡ
ΥϹΠϳΤΘϹΘΝΟϳΔΘΤΗΝΟϹΦΥΛΑΚΛΝϳ
ΛΝΧΟΜΝϳΟΛΤΘϳΔϳΛΡΩΤΩΤΟϳϹΟϹΟϳϹ

72 Page from a papyrus codex of the comedy "Dyscolus" by
   Menander, Geneva

73 Vellum page from the Codex Sinaiticus, London
   Page from a parchment codex of the "Iliad", Berlin

74 Page from a papyrus codex with parts of a Latin-Greek-Coptic
   conversation book, Berlin

The Coptic Book

Coptic was the last stage of development of Egyptian, and was spoken and written in the Christian era. In the late Ptolemaic era it took the place of New Egyptian as the popular language and is, in its origin, not the daughter but the sister of the literary and chancellery language, quite incorrectly called demotic (popular), which also stems from New Egyptian. The name "Coptic" originates from the Arabic spelling of the mutilated Greek word "Aigyptios" (Egyptian). It is not in speech but in writing that Coptic constitutes a breach in the curriculum vitae of the Egyptian language: Coptic uses Greek letters to which seven native vowel symbols were added to indicate those sounds not known in Greek. These symbols taken from demotic were adapted to the face of the Greek script, giving a uniform letter face. Thus Coptic has 31 symbols. Seen in relation to the mass, to say nothing of the complexity, of hieroglyphic, hieratic and demotic symbols and groups of symbols, this reduction denoted a great simplification. The greatest significance of Coptic writing, however, lies not so much in the simplification, but in the fact that for the first time in the history of Egyptian writing vowels were graphically reproduced. All pre-Coptic Egyptian writing was restricted to consonants.

Sporadic cautious attempts to transcribe Egyptian words and names with Greek letters date back to pre-Christian times. These are known as Old Coptic. But it is only after the 3rd century A.D. that the Coptic alphabet was used with consistency for writing, i.e. from the time when Coptic became a literary language. Although until a few years ago, early Christianity in Egypt was looked upon as having created Coptic as a literary language, an unexpected find of Gnostic original scripts in Coptic indicates that the Gnostics were its co-creators. The documents found in an earthenware vessel at Nag Hammadi (1946), the ancient Chenosboscion, roughly 66 miles north of Thebes, brought to light a whole library of Gnostic papyrus codices in Coptic. Those texts which have been published up till now show that these documents, the majority in the Sahidic dialect, have a very ancient character with regard to language. They are, in any case, older than the classical Coptic literary language which is most purely reproduced **78** in the translation of the New Testament and dated at about 400. During the 4th century the Egyptian followers

of Mani's teachings, the Manichaeans, developed an amazingly manifold activity in the field of translation which only became known through the sensational find at Medinet Madi in Al Fayyum (1930). The Manichaeans, too, did not use the classical language, but their own dialect.

All this indicates that Coptic was not a uniform language, but one that had several dialects. In general, Upper Egyptian and Lower Egyptian dialects can be distinguished. They are named Sahidic after the Arabic sa'id for Upper Country, and Bohairic after bohaira, Lower Country. These two dialects constitute the main part of Coptic literature. From the 3rd to the 10th centuries Sahidic was in use all over the country and became the classical written language at an early date. From the 11th century, however, it was displaced by Bohairic when Alexandria became the seat of the leader of the Egyptian Christians. Bohairic still survives in the liturgy of the Coptic Church. The Coptic documents which, in the **78** majority, date back to the 7th and 8th centuries and are almost non-existent in the 10th century show clearly that with the spreading of Islam, Arabic became the popular language. Two other Upper Egyptian dialects were called after the regions Akhmim and Asyut where they were spoken: Akhmimic and Asyutic (or Sub-Akhmimic) were only of local importance and had a much shorter life than the two main dialects. Asyutic or Sub-Akhmimic (the term is more or less conventional) is of importance in so far as the Manichaeans and, to a certain extent, the Gnostics used this dialect in their writings. Another local dialect developed at the oasis of Al Fayyum, but its literature was quite meagre and mainly written in one of the main dialects.

The Manichaean find of 1930 consisted of nine books containing a total of roughly 3,500 pages which were bought for the papyrus collection of the State Museums in Berlin and the Chester Beatty Collection in Dublin. Its **79** bad condition and losses due to the war have unfortunately resulted in the fact that only a small part of the total find has been scientifically evaluated. The Gnostic library of Nag Hammadi with its thirteen codices containing about 1,000 pages, of which 800 are well preserved, has brought to light at least 51 Gnostic and Hermetic manuscripts, some in more than one copy. Besides these texts there are three more Gnostic codices with Coptic scripts which were already known before the Nag Hammadi find, but which now rank behind the big Gnostic library as far as age, volume and importance are concerned. Another important papyrus find, probably also in Upper Egypt, which was made only a few years after the books of Nag Hammadi were discovered, consists of Greek and Coptic manuscripts of which the latter comprise more than 1,000 pages. The voluminous text material was bought mostly by the Bodmer Library, Geneva, Mississippi University and the Chester Beatty Collection.

Manichaeism and Gnosticism are, just as much as Christianity and Islam, typical book religions and, as such, they constitute an important chapter in the history of the Coptic book. Immediately after Manichaean manuscripts became known, they received a very favourable review by the famous "Papyrus Doctor of Berlin", Dr. Hugo Ibscher, who wrote:

"We may add the Manichaean manuscripts to the best products of Antiquity and they may well be compared with beautiful manuscripts of the Middle Ages and even with art printing of modern times. All Manichaean manuscripts are written with great care. All scribes—and there are several—were masters in their work. Letters are clear, distinct and run so fluidly that even today our spoiled eyes take pleasure in looking at them. The columns are well arranged, giving the codex page a pleasant appearance."

From the technical side, too, Manichaean manuscripts were produced with skill and care. The papyrus used for the codices was specially made for the purpose and not cut from a papyrus roll as was the case with all papyrus codices—Greek and Coptic—from earlier than the 4th century. The bindings of the Manichaean manuscripts have, unfortunately, been destroyed by unskilled handling.

The Nag Hammadi Gnostic manuscripts are in a far better state of preservation and we still can admire skilfully ornamented leather bindings. The leather binding gave sufficient protection because it ended in a flap which could be put around the open volume. The narrow sides also had flaps which could be secured by means of a leather strap. However, the make-up and the writing itself is not so regular as in the books of the Manichaeans. There are pages which are completely regular and others which have been written by negligent scribes who paid less attention to make-up and letter size than the Manichaean scribes.

If we named the Gnostics and Manichaeans as cocreators of the Coptic literary language, it must be said, however, that Christianity played a more dominating

ΝΑΤΩϢΒΕ ΜΝ ΤΑΝΑΠΑΥϹΙϹ ΝΑ
ΤϢΙΤϹ ΤΗ ΕΤΕΝΝΕΥΕϢϢΑ
ΧΕ ΕΡΟϹ ϨΝ ΝΑΙ ΩΝ ΤΗΡΟΥ Ν ΤΑΥ
ϢΩΠΕ ΜΝ ΝϹΑΝΑΙ ΜΝ ΝΕΥ
ΟϬΜ ΤΗΡΟΥ· ΝΑΙ ΔΕ ΤΗΡΟΥ Ν
ΤΑ ΕΙΧΟΟΥ ΕΡΩΤΝ Ν ϢΟΡΠ Α ΕΙ
ΧΟΟΥ ϢΑΝ ΤΕΤΝ Ρ ΟΥΟΕΙΝ ϨΜ
ΠΟΥΟΕΙΝ Ν ΖΩ ΟΕ ΝΑΥ· ΠΕΧΑ
ΝΑΥ ΝϬΙ ΜΑΡΙ ϨΑΜΜΗ ΧΕ ΠΧΟ
ΕΙϹ ΕΤΟΥΑΑΒ· ΝΕΚ ΜΑΘΗΤΗϹ Ν
ΤΑ ΗΕΙ ΤΩΝ Η ΕΥΝΑ ΒΩΚ ΤΩΝ Η ΕΥ
ΝΑ Ρ ΟΥ ΜΠΕΙΜΑ ΠΕΧΑΥ ΝΑΥ
ΝϬΙ ΠΤΕΛΙΟϹ Ν ϹΩΤΗΡ ΧΕ ΤΟΥ
ΩϢ ΕΤΡΕΤΝ ΕΙΜΕ ΧΕ ΤϹΟΦΙΑ
ΤΜΑΑΥ ΜΠΤΗΡΥ ΑΥΩ ΤΟΥ ΝΑϨ
ΤΟϹ ΑϬΡ ϨΝ ΑϹ ΙΤΟΟΤϹ ΜΠΙ
ΜΜΟϹ ΕΤΡΕΝ ϢϢΠΕ ΑϬΜ
ΠΕϹϨΟΟΥΤ ϨΜ ΠΕΤϨ ϨΝ ΑΥ ΔΕ
ΜΠΕΙΩΤ ΜΠΤΗΡΥ ΧΕ ΕΡΕΠΕ
ΑΓΑΘΟΝ ΟΥΩΝϨ ΕΒΟΛ ΑΥΜϹ
ΟΥΕΕΡΟΥ· ΑΥΤΑΜΙΟ ΜΠΕΙΚΑ
ΤΑΠΕΤΑϹΜΑ ΟΥΤΩΟΥ Ν ΝΙΑ
ΘΑΝΑΤΟϹ ΑΥΩ ΟΥΤΩΟΥ Ν ΗϹ
ΝΤΕΡΟΥ ϢΩΠΕ ΜΝ Ν ϹΑΝΗ
ΧΕ ΕΡΕΠ ΑΚΟΛΟΥΘΟΝ ΑΚΟΛΟΥ

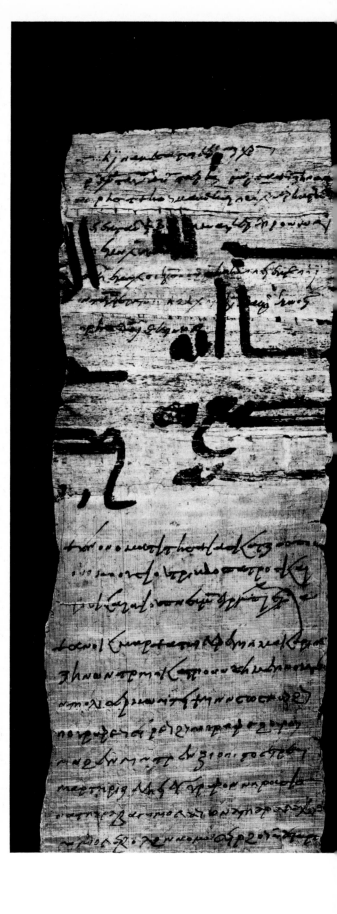

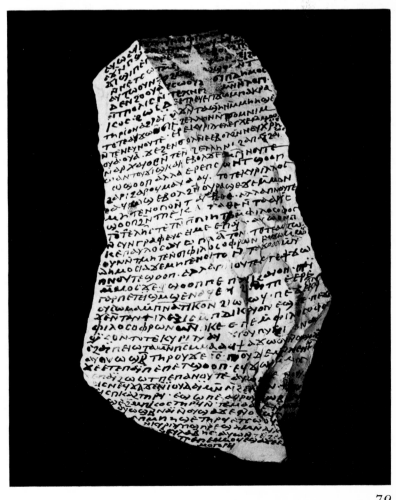

77 Leather binding from an Arabic Gospel
manuscript, Cairo

78 Leaf of a Coptic papyrus codex from Nag
Hammadi, Cairo
Coptic legal document on papyrus, Berlin

79 Sheet from the Coptic papyrus codex of
the Manichaean Kephalaia, Berlin
Sheet from the Coptic papyrus codex of
Proverbs, page 162, Berlin
Limestone fragment with the text of a
polemic conversation of Cyril, Berlin

First page of a Coptic parchment codex with the Book of the
Prophet Isaiah, Berlin

Title page from a Coptic parchment codex, Cairo

١٢٧ صورة تجلى ربنا يسوع المسيح وحضور موسى وايليا وخاطبانه وهنا وطرس ويعقوب ويوحنا لا يستطيعون النظر اليه

82 Two double pages from an illuminated Coptic-Arabic
collection of hymns, Cairo

83 Illuminated page from an Arabic Gospel manuscript, Cairo

84 Illuminated title page of the Acts of the Apostles, Cairo

الرسل المنتخبين

and numerically larger part in Coptic literature. Christian literature of mainly a hagiographical, homiletical and liturgical content started with the translation of the Holy Books of Christianity. Already about 250 A.D. Anthony of Koma, the father of the desert anchorites, heard the Gospel read in Coptic. In the middle of the 3rd century parts of the Bible were already translated into Coptic (Sahidic). In the 4th century the translation of the whole of the New Testament was probably completed. There is as yet no proof that the Old Testament was completely translated. Recently published sections of the Book of Joshua in Sahidic, showing traces of Akhmimic and Sub-Akhmimic influence, give rise to the hope that new finds will fill still existing gaps. The Psalms and Proverbs of Solomon from the Old Testament were particularly esteemed by the Copts. The Akhmimic Proverb codex in the German State Library, Berlin, the leather binding of which is ornamented with simple geometric lines and was reconstructed from preserved fragments, dates back, according to latest research, to the beginning of the 4th century. But proof has been provided that it has its origin in a Sahidic copy. The translation of psalms into Coptic probably dates back to the same age. The reading of psalters was obligatory for the Pachomian monks.

The monasteries became and have remained the places where Coptic literature and Coptic books were cultivated and developed. The most prominent representative of Coptic national literature, Apa Schenute of Atripe (died about 450) was for a long time abbot of the White Monastery near Sohag in Upper Egypt. Although Schenute's

writings bear a practical and worldly trait—Christian Coptic literature cannot, and does not want to, deny its monastic origin. Biblical and monastic subjects dominated in popular poetry, which had its golden age at about 1000.

A good insight into a Coptic monastery may be gained from the manuscripts—now in the British Museum—of the library which was discovered in 1910 in the grounds of the old monastery in Hamouli in the southern part of Al Fayyum. The collection consists of more than fifty codices from every branch of church literature and most of them are ornamented with a front picture. The earliest manuscripts date back to the first half of the 9th century.

A rich collection of Coptic manuscripts from the White Monastery near Sohag are to be found in the Pierpont Morgan Library in New York. This collection is unique with regard to its good state of preservation. Most of the volumes are written in Sahidic and can be dated back to approximately the 9th century. Monks of this monastery were careful scribes and knew how to make several kinds of ink. Many inkpots reminiscent of those of Pharaonic times were found in the vicinity of the monastery.

Peter of Dronka, a skilful scribe who lived in the monastery of Amba Anthonius near the Red Sea, is said to have been a specialist in making ink. There were a hundred scribes in this monastery who, in groups of ten, had each specialised in copying certain definite types of manuscripts. They worked on copies to be used in the churches of Egypt.

From its very inception the Coptic book took the codex form which had already been largely determined by the

79

Christian literature in Greek. During the course of the centuries papyrus was increasingly displaced by parchment and finally by paper. It is clear that considerable differences exist with regard to the size and make-up of the books. As a rule the leaves, most of which bear a page number, have only one column; rarely two or more narrow ones. Large initials, moved out to the left, added to the beauty of the writing picture as did the signs 80 for separating paragraphs: paragraphos, coronis and diple, some of which are calligraphical masterpieces. Red ink was often used for titles and beginnings of chapters. The colours known from early times were used for the various decorative forms; for braid patterns, geometric patterns 81 and flower patterns, for rosettes and crosses. And in increasing measure Coptic and, later on, Coptic-Arabic books show pictures of saints and angels, birds and animals.

Special care was given to the illustration of biblical scenes and hagiographical subjects. 82, 83,

In monasteries of Wadi Natrum, as for instance in Abu 84 Makkar, the skilful scribes were monks who were able to make several kinds of ink and colours and carry out artistic book-binding work. Sometimes they were even 77 accused of alchemy. Several stamps for ornaments on bindings have been found there and also silver boxes in which valuable manuscripts could be safely kept. Some of these boxes are to be seen in the Coptic Museum in Cairo.

In the decor there is a similarity between Coptic crosses and those found in early Celtic manuscripts. After the Irish had taken their model of monastic life from Egypt, they took the Egyptian books as models for their own. Thus the make-up of Coptic books influenced, in the last instance, early medieval book illumination in Europe.

Captions to the Illustrations

76 *Sheet from the Coptic parchment codex of the Cambyses story*. The Cambyses story is one of the very rare narrative secular books of Coptic literature. It depicts Egyptian resistance after the Persian (Sassanidic) and perhaps also the Arab conquest of the country. The preserved part of the Berlin manuscript consists of 6 sheets. Staatliche Museen zu Berlin, Papyrus-Sammlung P 9009. Parchment; 19 × 15.5 cms (single sheet)

77 *Leather binding from an Arabic Gospel manuscript*. The coloured binding shows a rich decor of winding tendrils and stylized blossoms.
Coptic Museum, Cairo, Cat. No. 127, Liturgy 16, formerly 75.
Leather, 14.5 × 10 cms.
Egypt, presented by the Coptic Patriarchate, 1613

78 *Leaf of a Coptic papyrus codex from Nag Hammadi*. The very carefully written page shows the page number 114 at top and is from codex III containing the "Sophia of Jesus Christ" from page 90, 14—119, 18.
Coptic Museum, Cairo, Cat. No. 10544, Gnostic 114. Papyrus; 17 × 37 cms.
Chenoboscion near Nag Hammadi, 4th century A.D.

78 *Coptic legal document on papyrus*. A document testifying to the sale of a house on a long, narrow papyrus roll for which 12 sheets are glued together. With the exception of the first sheet with the Arabic record, the writing is at right angles to the fibres. The text of the document contains 154 lines on the recto, and the two last lines show the Greek signature of the scribe. On the verso 2 lines are in Greek and 7 in Coptic. The contract consists of a vertically rolled column. The illustration shows the beginning of the document with the

Arabic record. Staatliche Museen zu Berlin, Papyrus-Sammlung P 10606. Papyrus; 232 × 14 cms. Djeme (Thebes) 8th century. W. E. Crum and G. Steindorff, Koptische Rechtsurkunden des achten Jahrhunderts aus Djeme (Thebes), 1st Vol., Leipzig 1912, No. 24

79 *Sheet from the Coptic papyrus codex of the Manichaean Kephalaia*. According to H. Ibscher, the papyrus restorer, the complete codex—acquired in part by the State Museums in Berlin and in part by the Chester Beatty Collection, Dublin—consisted of roughly 750 pages and was bound in quires, each with 6 double sheets. Every sheet had the page number and the quire number in the top margin, to the left and right respectively, with the title in the centre. Staatliche Museen zu Berlin, Papyrus-Sammlung P 15996 Papyrus; 31.5 × 18 cms. Medinet Madi (Fayyum), beginning of the 5th century A.D. H. J. Polotsky and A. Böhlig, Manichäische Handschriften der Staatlichen Museen Berlin, Vol. 1, Kephalaia (1. Hälfte); with an article by H. Ibscher, Stuttgart 1940; A. Böhlig, Vol. 1, Kephalaia (2. Hälfte, Lief. 11/12), Stuttgart 1966; by the same author, Aus den manichäischen "Kephalaia des Lehrers", Wiss. Zeitschrift der Martin-Luther-Universität Halle-Wittenberg V (1956) G, pages 1067—84; Translation of codex pages 244—291 (6. Doppellieferung)

79 *Sheet from the Coptic papyrus codex of Proverbs, page 162*. The codex, which is almost quadratic in format, consists of 40 double and 3 single sheets bound in one section. The 162 written pages are numbered at the top and the Proverbs are separated by horizontal lines in the left margin. The single sheets of the codex were covered with chiffon silk by Dr. R. Ibscher in 1958/59 and bound by W. Kiessig, who

also reconstructed the binding after preserved remains of the original. Deutsche Staatsbibliothek, Berlin, Ms. or. oct. 987. Papyrus; 12.5×approx. 25 cms. Found at the Dei Schedeh monastery near Akhmim; early 4th century A.D. A. Böhlig, Der achmimische Proverbientext nach Ms. Berol. orient. oct. 987. Part I: Text und Rekonstruktion der sahidischen Vorlage (Studien zur Erforschung d. christl. Ägyptens, Heft 3) München 1958. With a description of the manuscript by H. Ibscher. Proverbiencodex (Facsimile edition), Verlag Edition Leipzig, 1963, with an epilogue by A. Böhlig.

79 *Limestone fragment with the text of a polemic conversation of Cyril.* This is the largest limestone fragment bearing Coptic writing. The text covers the recto and the verso and reports on a polemic conversation between the young Christian Cyril and a Greek philosopher on the existence of pagan Gods. It is probably a legend from the life of the famous Patriarch Cyril of Alexandria (early 5th century A.D.). Staatliche Museen zu Berlin, Papyrus-Sammlung, P 14763. Limestone; 39 × approx. 32 cms. Probably from Thebes, about 5th century A.D. F. Hintze and S. Morenz, Ein Streitgespräch Kyrills, ZÄZ 79 (1954), page 125 and following

80 *First page of a Coptic parchment codex with the Book of the Prophet Isaiah.* These pages originally belonged to a double sheet of a large and beautifully arranged parchment codex of a manuscript from the Old Testament. Perhaps this book also contained the books of other prophets. Every page is written in two columns with red initials and with page numbers at the top on the outside edge. The illustration shows page 1 with the title surrounded by a coloured braid pattern which runs out to a diple on the left and right. The margins are formed at the left by a coronis and a paragraphos ornamented with stylized blossoms which reaches to the right-hand column. Staatliche Museen zu Berlin, Papyrus-Sammlung P 11966. Parchment, size of the double sheet 35×54 cms. From the Library of the Hamuli Monastery (Fayyum) about 10th century A.D.

81 *Title page from a Coptic parchment codex.* This title page of the Gospel of St. John with prologue, which is richly decorated with coloured interweaving patterns and stylized blossoms, is part of a parchment manuscript of the four Gospels in Bohairic. Coptic Museum, Cairo, Cat. No. 156, Biblical 32, formerly 104. Parchment; 27×22.5 cms. Egypt; presented by the Coptic Patriarchate; 13th century

82 *Double page from an illuminated Coptic-Arabic collection of hymns.* The coloured illustration of the top half of the double page—which strangely enough shows two different page numbers—shows Adam on the left and Eve on the right. They are both in the Garden of Eden surrounded by animals. Eve has already succumbed to the temptations of the serpent, and she and Adam, clad with fig-leaf skirts, are picking fruit

from the tree of knowledge. The Coptic text of this collection of hymns in honour of the Virgin Mary on the lower half of the sheet is written with great care and has large set-out initials with a serpent on the left as coronis. The text is surrounded by a border which separates the Coptic from the Arabic text and includes an indication that the hymn is meant for the second day of the week. Coptic Museum, Cairo, Cat. No. 2741, Liturgy 159, formerly 358. Cloth paper; 16×11 cms. Egypt; 18th century

82 *Double page from an illuminated Coptic-Arabic collection of hymns.* The double page shows the same scene, but here Adam and Eve have a halo and on the left God's arm points down from a cloud indicating the expulsion from paradise. On the same page, and next to the Coptic script, the illuminator depicted the crowned Virgin Mary with her right hand raised in blessing. This hymn was also for the second day of the week. Coptic Museum, Cairo, Cat. No. 4180, Liturgy 177, formerly 418. Cloth paper; 11.5×8.5 cms. Egypt; Acquired Nov. 11, 1942; 19th century

83 *Illuminated page from an Arabic Gospel manuscript.* The transfiguration of Christ according to the New Testament is shown in two dimensions. Below the disciples Peter, John and Jacob on a mountain—above them in a cloud the transfigurated Jesus being addressed by Moses with the decalogue (left) and the Prophet Elijah (right). Mountains in the background indicate a landscape and hatchings stress the radiance and elevation of the transfigurated. Coptic Museum, Cairo, Cat. No. 732, Liturgy 27, formerly 99. Cloth paper; 19×14.5 cms. Egypt; Presented by St. Mark's Cathedral, 1689

84 *Illuminated title page of the Acts of the Apostles.* The coloured title page of the Acts is part of a larger codex; in the heading left it bears the page number 158. The picture shows the Virgin Mary amongst the archangels and apostles and above her Christ with four angels. The few lines of the text are in Arabic. Coptic Museum, Cairo, Cat. No. 146, Biblical 23, formerly 94. Cloth paper; 23.5×16.5 cms. Egypt; Presented by the Coptic Patriarchate; 1249

85 *Illuminated page from the Arabic Gospel manuscript.* It shows the scene of the raising of Lazarus from the dead according to St. John 11. In the right half of the picture is Jesus, who has just performed the miracle, together with three disciples; to the left of Jesus are Mary and Martha, the two sisters of Lazarus with two men behind them. On the extreme left is Lazarus, who has risen from the dead and, still swathed like a mummy in his shrouds, stands in front of his opened grave inclined in front of him. The picture is framed with a double line and the head of the sheet carries a line of Arabic text.
Coptic Museum, Cairo, Cat. No. 151, Liturgy 27, formerly 99. Cloth paper; 13×8.5 cms.
Egypt; 1689

The Book in Islamic Egypt

Arabic—The New Unifying Language

With the year of the Hegira (higra) 622, the face of the Near East began to change enormously. The Prophet Mohammed preached submission to the will of Allah (Islam) to the tribes of the Arabian peninsula—and he was listened to. In the ten years that followed the voluntary flight from Mecca in 622, the original small and persecuted flock of believers created the basis for the future caliphate in Medina. The following Holy War carried out by the tribes which had been converted to Islam did not lead straight away to the Arabization of the conquered territories. After the sudden death of Mohammed in 632 four of his closest collaborators succeeded each other as caliphs (successors) and exercised religious and state leadership. In the struggle for succession which soon started, the Omayyads won the upper hand and guided the destinies of the world empire until 750 through good and bad times. Only when they had arrived at the zenith of their power at the beginning of the 8th century was Arabic declared the official language. Until that time the Islamic-Egyptian administrative authorities *101* had used Greek together with Arabic, as can be seen from the tax order issued by Qurra ibn Sarik in 709/710. In Iraq the Persian language tradition lived on through Pahlavi. The most important of the Omayyads, Abdal-Malik (686—705) and his eldest son al Walid (705—15), put an end to this and thus Arabic became the leading language of the Near East.

Arabic is one of the Semitic languages. A number of these languages—among them Arabic—have no graphic reproduction of the vowels. There are 28 consonants which are written from the right to the left and form the skeleton of the words. Unlike our languages Arabic knows no difference between handwritten and printed scripts, although abbreviations in handwriting later came into being. The Arabic alphabet has its origin in the Nabataean script. The Nabataean kingdom—its centre was east of the Jordan—had already been annexed by the Emperor Trajan in 106 A.D., but due to continued trading activities its script spread to the north and the south. Petra, the capital of the kingdom, deserves special mention. Together with Arabic the Nabataean language belongs to a sub-group of the Semitic languages. Trade caused the Nabataeans to develop a cursive script which

they inscribed in stone and probably other materials as well. The monumental inscription at Namarah (328) opened the door for the development of an Arabic script. In these times the trading Arabs contented themselves with the Nabataean script which had 24 consonants; but since their language had 28 consonants, 4 new signs had to be invented. In addition to this, inscribing on stones brought about such a marked simplification that 9 signs expressed 20 consonants. Landmarks for the development of Arabic writing are the trilingual (Syriac, Arabic and Greek) Zebed inscription dated 512 A.D. and the bilingual (Arabic, Greek) inscription of Harran, dated 568 A.D. The Arabic letters of the latter have a great similarity to Nabataean cursive writing still in use on the Sinai peninsula. Later, this writing became the model for the Kufic script.

After Islam had spread over the Near East and North Africa, and the work of administration grown accordingly, it became necessary to have a script that was not open to misinterpretation. Although in the early Islamic times the Arabs maintained the old form, they began, analogous to the Syrian script, to distinguish those twenty signs which could easily be mistaken by using dots, the so-called diacritical points. Without diacritical dots are stone inscriptions, e.g. on the tombstone of Ibn Hair in Cairo from 652, also the papyri. In Islamic times the makers of the papyrus rolls glued on one sheet at the beginning which contained the faith formula: "In the name of Allah, the Merciful, the Compassionate. There is no god but Allah, Mohammed is his prophet." They also added this formula to rolls with a Christian content. For these protocols a stamp was used with the result that the exact form of the signs suffered. And, of course, no reading signs were added. The protocol shown in the illustration dates back to the beginning of the 8th century. Above a line of Arabic text there are two lines of Greek translation. *102* The thick strokes at the end of the Greek lines are filling marks. The pass for a village inhabitant, written *102* a little later, shows a strikingly clear script, but the distinguishing dots are missing completely. The inconsistency with which such a process can develop may be gauged from the bilingual tax order of Qurra which *101* shows a number of diacritical dots, even though it was written much earlier. In later times, scholars no longer

Burial stele of Ibn Hair, limestone, Cairo

quarrelled about the diacritical signs which had become part of the written language, but about the auxiliary signs for brief vowels. Arabic has only 3 vowels: a, i and u. Long vowels were expressed through the semi-consonants Alif (ā), Waw (ū) and Ya (ī) and were thus not liable to misinterpretation. The frequency with which short vowels were used varies in the manuscripts—some are vowelized throughout. One of the greatest teachers of law, Malik ibn Anas (d. 795) prohibited the use of these signs. Today, these signs are only used in passages in books where unpleasant confusion could occur. The Koran is an exception; since early Islamic times its copies have been vowelized in order to limit the number of possible interpretations.

Writing Materials

The large increase in Islamic book production becomes quite clear on taking a look at the writing materials. Our knowledge is based on Islamic tradition and on excavations in Egypt. Writing materials are mentioned in Arab sources dealing with the collection of Koran texts by Said ibn Thabit in the year 12 (633—634 A.D.) for the first caliph Abu Bakr. The Koran itself also contains references to these materials.

The "fihrist" of Ibn al-Nadim (987 A.D.) lists leather scraps (rikā), limestone slabs (likhaf), palm bark ('usub), shoulder blades (aktaf) and wooden boards as writing materials used by the Arabs. According to tradition Said ibn Thabit wrote his collection for Abu Bakr on leather scraps, shoulder blades and palm bark.

It is only natural that the Islamic conquerors used the same writing materials as the Egyptians. Firstly to be named is the flexible papyrus, which was both popular and expensive and had been in use in the Mediterranean area since Pharaonic times. From Egypt the use of papyrus spread to the whole of the ancient world. Islamic officials in Egypt used this material until the 13/14th centuries. Important finds of Arabic papyri have been made at Ehnas (Heracleopolis Magna), El Behnesa (Oxyrhynchus), El Ashmunain (Hermopolis Magna) and Kom Eshqauh (Aphrodite) in Upper Egypt. Arabic papyri are preserved in libraries and museums all over the world; there are about 8,000 in the Archduke Rainer Collection in Vienna and more than 2,000 in Egypt in the National Library (Dar al Kutub) in Cairo. This material tells us about living conditions in Egypt during the Middle Ages. In other parts of the caliphate paper had long since taken over the leading role. The Caliph Omayyad al-Walid I (705—715) is said to be the first to have written on papyrus. It was also during his era that the previously mentioned protocol (the Islamic faith formula with Greek translation) was written. Leather was also known and appreciated as a writing material by the predecessors of the conquering Muslims.

In the eyes of the followers of Islam, Copts were "book people", i.e. they had a book as basis for their faith. For these books they needed a suitable and durable writing material. Besides papyrus they used also expensive, but less appreciated, parchment. The size of the tanned goat skins called for the codex form. The Greeks, however, considered the book roll to be the only elegant form. As described in the development of the Coptic book in the previous chapter, Egyptian Christians also used papyrus codices. The Muslims used parchment only for important documents and the Koran; the codex became the dominating book form and then the papyrus. The Egyptian National Library has one of the most important papyrus codices: "Collection of the Tradition" by Abdallah ibn Wahb (died 812); it was written in the second half of the 9th century 112 and found at Edfu in 1922.

In addition there was also untanned leather, which was dyed red-brown and rolled like papyrus. The roll was bound by a strip of leather and was used for trade affairs. Other writing material like limestone ostraca, potsherd ostraca and wooden boards were hardly used by the conquerors. Palm leaf panicles and bones (shoulder blades and ribs) of camels had to suffice for brief notes, and also for the first copies of the Koran. The Europeans of the Middle Ages considered the Muslims to be the inventors of paper, but it is, of course, a much earlier Chinese discovery. The Muslims had heard of the Chinese paper production, which had been kept secret, when they extended their campaigns of conquest to Central Asia. In a war against two quarrelling princes in Horasan at about 750 the general who had been charged with bringing order to the country chased the princes, who had concluded pacts with China, as far as the Chinese frontier and was able to take some prisoners experienced in paper making; he had them settled in Samarkand. In the years that followed a flourishing paper making industry developed there and from Samarkand paper spread over the whole Islamic world. The names of the various kinds of paper were derived from those of the patrons of the manufacturers. It seems, however, that the first was named Pharaonic paper (quirtas fir'auni)— papyrus and paper can be named with one word in Arabic—in contrast to the Egyptian papyrus (quirtas Misri). It was only 50 years later that the art of paper making spread from Samarkand to Baghdad, the capital of the Abbasid empire. The first paper mill is said to have been built about 750 under the special protection of the Barmecides, the highly-gifted family of state servants in the service of the Caliph Harun al-Rashid (786—809), known from "The Arabian Nights".

One of these papers is named after the Grand Vizier Ja'far of the Barmecide family. The first paper book was published in Baghdad in 870. From the 11th century onwards paper making spread beyond Egypt. Prior to this time the Egyptian authorities had imported paper from Samarkand; the oldest Egyptian writings on paper date back to the years 796—818. At the end of the 12th century the learned physician and naturalist al Bagdadi (d. 1231) wrote that the people of Cairo collected rags to sell them to the paper mills. During the 14th century the Islamic paper monopoly was broken by European competition, just as three centuries earlier papyrus production had been superseded by Samarkand paper.

Arabic uses the Latin loanword qalam (calamus) for pen, and the Islamic scribes used a hard, closed reed which they roasted and afterwards watered. Inks were also part of the scribe's utensils—black ink from lampblack and red from cinnobar which were mixed in small bowls as in the olden days. The ink used for writing on papyrus was very much like Chinese ink. In China it was prepared by placing a number of lighted wicks in a vessel filled with oil over which was placed a funnel-shaped iron hood. When this hood was coated black, the lampblack was brushed off, collected on paper and mixed with a solution of gum or gluten: there was no great difference in Arabic ink. Kalkashandi (d. 1418) wrote in detail about the production of ink in both liquid and powder form. Honey, salt, gum and gallnuts were added to the lampblack.

Islamic Egypt played an important role in preparing block printing (wooden plate print). The papyrus collection of the Austrian National Library in Vienna has some fragments of book printing from Egypt, dating from between 900 and 1350. The art of block printing was probably brought to Eygpt from China by the first Mongols. And from Egypt it spread to the Western world.

The Holy Book—The Koran

Codification and Calligraphy

The Koran is the Holy Book of the Islamic world. The Koran, which can be translated as "the recitation", was not available in a codified form at the death of the Prophet. For the Muslims the Koran is the revealed word of Allah. The revelations are known as suras (chapters) and consist of verses. There are suras with three and some with over 200 verses. Whereas the older suras are written in a powerful rhythmic, rhetorically impressive rhymed prose, the later ones, particularly the Medinan suras, are more narrative. The subject matter is diverse: from prayers for protection to legal instructions. Several verses deal with the personal life of the Prophet. The many texts permit a deep insight into the social problems and philosophical thought of the era. The revelations of the Prophet were first written down by his secretaries who then arranged the longest suras at the beginning and the shortest at the end. They have no chronological order. It has been found that of the 114 canonic suras the shortest are the oldest. The prosaic long suras regulated the state life of the growing community. After the Prophet's death the Islamic Tradition had four versions in circulation and not all of them had the same number of suras. The third successor of Mohammed, Caliph Uthman, had several copies of the version based on Mohammed with 114 suras edited and written up by a commission consisting of Zaiyd ibn Thabit, Abd Allah ibn al Zubair, Said ibn al Asi and Abd al Rahman ibn al Harith. These copies were then sent to the most important cities of provinces. The work of the meritorious apostles of the Prophet was accepted by the community. As a result of the disputes about the successor to the leadership of the community and the internal struggles for power it was, however, impossible to prevent a split in the community. During these struggles Caliph Uthman was murdered.

At this junction the question of dissemination arose. The Muslims had entered Egypt in 639 and conquered the Byzantine province at one swoop; here they received significant impulses for the administration and books. In Egypt they came into close contact with the Coptic church, one of the powerful Christian national churches whose Holy Books existed in codex form partly on papyrus and partly on parchment. The best vehicle for the spreading of the Koran was durable parchment. It is possible that this idea came from the Eastern churches, of which the Christian Coptic Church of Egypt was one.

In this connection we must clearly emphasize the importance of Egypt for early Islam. The caliph had copies of the Koran made in the capital Medina and had them sent to the mosques in the large cities. It also became the custom to deposit other copies at these places. In this way libraries attached to the mosques developed; these became educational centres where young people were taught to recite and read the Koran and were introduced to a study of philosophy and of Hadith.

Such an important book also deserved a special hand. In the early Islamic period there were two types of writing—the Kufic and the Naskhi. The first was derived from the monumental and ornamental writing of the Nabataeans which appeared angular and stiff as it was carved into stone and embossed on coins. The name is derived from the town of Kufa, founded by the victorious Muslims in Southern Iraq in 638. A short time later this city became one of the spiritual centres of Islam. Today it is no longer possible to say whether the stone script was reproduced on parchment at this place. The script used for reproducing the "Book of Books" is decorative and noble. In the Islamic countries, where it is highly esteemed, the art of calligraphy has developed from modest beginnings right up to our day. Since many theologians and pious Muslims were, from the very beginning, hostile to figural representation and painting, calligraphy was considered an art of great importance.

To start with, this art was largely limited to the Holy Book. The Koran copyists changed little in the letter form which had developed in stone. The straight line dominates, curved lines are seldom seen. The parchment codex of the 7th century in the Egyptian National Library demonstrates this well. Despite its ragged edges this script is not ungraceful. One can feel that an effort towards ornamentation has been made. The letters gained in balance and beauty the more the copyists became familiar with their materials. In the 8th century those round letters which led to a fatal stiffness in the ornamentation came into being. The example from the 8th century—also in the *106* Egyptian National Library—already shows these traits. In the 9th century when writing had slowly grown into calligraphical flourishes—they corrupted the archaic character of the script. Calligraphers swung the lower end of the simple vertical stroke, the semi-consonant Alif, towards the right, i.e. in opposition to the direction of writing. This small example is intended to indicate to which extent one could deviate from script character to *106* ornament. The 10th century brought little that was new to Kufic. The copies were more or less good imitations without new variations. Calligraphers' creative talent concentrated on flourished script. The example from the Freer Gallery, Washington, still stands comparison with foregoing centuries, but there are already incorrect copies. In the 11th century Kufic disappeared from copyist traditions.

108

The seriousness with which calligraphy was pursued can be gauged from the fact that highly educated people occupied themselves with the art, and princes added to their fame through having a beautiful handwriting. After Kufic had been banned in the copying of the Koran, its place was taken by a fully developed cursive script (Naskhi). The scribes used it for business transactions and the production of secular books. All codices by famous scholars of the Islamic world were written in this form. It was a simple type of script with a clear consonant body whose main advantage was that it could be read by all literates. In addition, it was quite easy to copy on all kinds of writing materials; it was of no matter whether one wrote on papyrus, parchment or palm bark. The new and practicable paper was adapted to parchment by smoothing and dyeing. The coming into general use of paper brought with it a change in the calligraphy; from the early Abbasid era a flourished cursive script took a leading place. The Islamic tradition has many different scripts but no copies are preserved. The calligraphers had strict rules for Naskhi script: ascenders and descenders had a fixed relation to the body of the letter; height and width were also proportionate. The nine forms for the twenty consonants in Arabic were varied by down-strokes or special diacritical signs which conformed to calligraphic rules. The Vizier Ibn Muqla (d. 940) is said to have played a leading role in the displacement of Kufic and to have written in a clear Naskhi script although the copy attributed to him has proved to be a falsification of a later date. The writer Ali ibn Sbaida ar-Rihani (d. 834) developed a variation of the Naskhi script which received his name. He developed his script from the Thuluth in which letter height and width of strokes are only one third of the old Kufic script. This can be clearly observed in the width of the strokes. In both variations the vertical stroke of the Alif is longer than in the normal form. The sloping down-strokes of both variations vary in that one runs to a point and the other is cut off at a diagonal. An example of Rihani script is a copy of the Koran for the Sultan Mu'ayyad at the beginning of the 15th century; an example of Thuluth script is a sheet from the Freer Gallery in Washington. Among the most important works on the art of calligraphy is "Umdat al Kuttah wa Uddat

111

110

dhawi l-albab" by al-Mu'izz Ibn Badis, Prince of Tunis (d. 1061). It deals at length with the tools and aids used in the art of calligraphy. Al Kalkashandi, Al Nadim, and Tashkuprizada (d. 1560) with his "Miftah al-Saadi", devote several chapters to calligraphy and calligraphers. Ibn Muqla (d. 940) also wrote a treatise on calligraphy, which was considered a special section of the copying work carried out by the scribes. The Arabic term "Wirakah" applies to the copying of books as well as book-binding and bookselling. The "Warrakah" were papermakers, copyists and book-binders and they also supplied writing materials. Gilders who ornamented the pages and especially book-bindings collaborated with copyists as well as with book-binders who produced beautiful leather bindings. The great masters were acquainted with all three kinds of work; therefore it is possible for a complete book to be the work of one person. The art of copying was a gainful activity in the Islamic world. In the libraries copyists were employed to copy manuscripts; writers, too, worked as copyists. The great mathematician and optician Ibn al Haythem transcribed Arabic copies of Euclid and sold them. Often attached to the workshops were bookshops which soon became meeting places for the educated classes. Calligraphical masterpieces were esteemed and for rare pieces high prices had to be paid. The Mameluke historian Al-Maqrizi reports that a copy of the historical works of Al-Tabari, which had several volumes, cost 100 dinars. It was possible to rent a tavern for twelve months for one dinar. The average price of a book was one to two dinars. The high price for Al-Tabari's work arose from the fact that it consisted of several volumes; it was also an expression of the estimation in which the writer was held. Some of the Koran copyists have achieved special fame. Among them the most famous master after Ibn Muqla is Ibn al-Bawwab, who died in Baghdad in 1032. He is said to have made 500 copies of the Koran. From an 11th century source we know that a professional scribe was able to copy about 100 pages a day, but it is certain that he could not endure such physical strain day in, day out. Even if Ibn al-Bawwab's performance seems a little exaggerated—he was the head of a school for calligraphers— it does, nevertheless, testify to the fertility of his labours.

109

The beautiful manuscript in the Chester Beatty Library, Dublin, eloquently demonstrates his skill. The last of these masters is Yakut al Mustasmi (d. 1298) whose pupils were mainly Persians. He introduced the diagonally cut reed pen and used the classic Naskhi script. The Egyptian National Library possesses a manuscript written by him in 1290. With the cultural decline in Iraq the centre moved to

111

Persia and Egypt and soon special schools developed in these countries. The Arabic-Egyptian school promoted traditional styles and attained good results. In the 14th century the chief calligrapher of Egypt was Abd al-Rahman ibn Saigh (d. 1441) who copied the Koran in 60 days for the Sultan Barkuk (reigned from 1382—1398). This copy is now in the possession of the Egyptian National Library.

Book-bindings

The learned philologist and writer Al-Jahiz (d. 886) reports that Abyssinians introduced the codex or bound book to the Muslims. Be that as it may, one can assume with certainty that the Arabs were acquainted with the codex from Christian churches in Syria, Palestine and Egypt at the beginning of the 7th century. Islamic book production really started only after the great conquests had been concluded. The experience of Egypt must have contributed to this fact.

Islamic scribes kept the classic format of the codex sheets: they were rectangular, but the relationship of height to width was less than a normal page of the present time. Both papyrus and parchment was cut to this size and they could be used in wide or upright format. The single sheets were gathered together into quires and bound in leather. Only a few examples of the art of book-binding from the early Islamic era are still in existence. A thin wooden board or papyrus mâché, over which beautifully worked leather was spanned, served as the basis of a book cover. In the Coptic monastery libraries a number of codices with leather bindings have survived the centuries of crusades and Mongol campaigns.

Islamic sources tell us much about leather processing and the places where it was produced. The fame of the Yemenites was greater than that of any other leather centre in pre-Islamic times, and it seems that there was little change in early Islamic times. From then on the leather artisans at the oasis of Al Taif slowly became dangerous competitors. In the 12th century tanners emigrated from there to Egypt and settled in a particular quarter near the town wall of Old Cairo. The Mameluke historian Al-Maqrizi tells us that they introduced the great tradition of the Egyptian book-binding art in the 14th and 15th centuries.

103,104, The leather was often coloured, as our examples show. 105 For linear ornaments the book-binder used a knife or a whet iron with which he could engrave three parallel lines at once. Punched designs were also a popular form of ornamentation. The centre-pieces or the margins were emphasized through decorative painting. During the heyday of Egyptian book-binding gold was used lavishly; the pieces reproduced here have gilded punched lines. Leather, sometimes in various colours, was cut into strips and plaited to form edgings. Punched filigree leather was often laid over material of a different colour. In Coptic bindings appliqué is also met with, for instance, a leather net applied to a gilded background.

It goes without saying that such costly bindings were only used for precious codices, above all, for copies of the Koran. For the most part they were the property of the larger libraries whose stock had been collected under the patronage of the various potentates and which, through the course of time, were almost completely destroyed. A number of the book-binders were employed at the famous libraries. The services of a well-known and coveted master book-binder enhanced the reputation of a library just as much as those of a master copyist. Others had their own workshops or worked in the bookshops which were responsible for all work connected with the book trade. The examples reproduced are from the late Egyptian heyday. Apart from these only Coptic bindings from the early times are known from Egypt. They would not have differed much from Islamic bindings, because we know that the Muslims had some of their books bound in Coptic monasteries. At this time, however, the centres of Islamic culture were still outside Egypt, on the Iberian peninsula and in Iraq.

The Contents of the Books

Theology

Mohammed left only the Koran to his rapidly growing community. With it his successors, the caliphs, were to guide the political and religious life of the Islamic peoples. Soon, however, quarrels broke out about the interpretation of contested texts which were used by the individual pretender to the office of caliph as a theological basis for his claim. According to the Islamic concept the ultimate truth lies with the Prophet and countless of his utterances on law and religion were known to his followers. At first the theologians of Medina—to whence Mohammed had flown from Mecca in 622—recorded these texts with the name of the transmitter. Thus the prophetic Tradition (Hadith) came into being. The first works that proceed from this base deal with the life of the Prophet, the "Book of the Beginning" (Kitab al-Mubtada by Ibn Isha, d. 768) and the wars of the Prophet, the "Book of the Campaigns" (Kitab al-Magazi by Al-Asadi, d. 758). The Traditions and their transmitters did not, as a result of the enormous increase in the material, remain uncontested. According to their respective religious orientation, theologians, lawyers and historians looked for, or even invented, a text that suited their purpose. At the beginning of the 9th century two theologians, al-Bukhari (d. 870) and Muslim (d. 875), started scrutinizations and research work. Al-Bukhari is said to have looked through 600,000 traditions and their hereditary line and to have immediately been able to distinguish between true and false. He issued a collection of "authoritative" texts which was canonized at a later stage. Muslim proceeded in a similar manner and issued a collection which was also canonized. During the period in which this specific Islamic science matured Abd Ibn Wahb (d. 812) wrote in Egypt his "Collection of the Traditions" (Kitab al-Jami fil-hadith). In Egypt, the Governor Abd-al Aziz ibn Marwan (d. 704) promoted such research. And Urwa ibn al-Zubayr, head of the theological school in Medina, is said to have influenced Marwan's decision during his visit to Egypt in 680. The caliphate, which had reached the zenith of its power in the 8th and 9th centuries, had need of a unified system of administration of justice based on the Islamic religion. Logically, jurisprudence based itself on the Koran and the written Tradition (Hadith). The four most famous jurists were Abu Hanifi (d. 767), Malik ibn Anas (d. 795), al-Shafi'i (d. 820) and Ibn Hanbal (d. 855). The Shafi'i school prevailed in Egypt and is still valid in the religious sphere today. The ultimate dogmatic and ethical formation of theology took place at the end of the 10th century. The invasions of the Crusaders and later Mongols that then set in put an end to the fruitful intellectual development. From that time until into the 15th century the main attention of the spiritual leaders was limited to commentaries and compilations of the canonic works of their predecessors.

History

The interest of the Islamic world in the significant events which occurred under the first four caliphs, the immediate successors to Mohammed, caused the scholars to write detailed records of the conquests and administration in an annalistic, and not historio-critical, sense. The only source the historians had were the Traditions. As early as the 9th century the world on the Nile, which was so rich in tradition, tempted Ibn Abd al-Hakam (d. 871) to write down all that was worth knowing about the "Conquest of Egypt, North Africa and Spain". At about the same time al-Baladuri (d. 892) was working on his book about the Islamic "Conquest of the Countries" (Futuh al-Buldan). This was followed by the "Annals" of Ibn Jarir al-Tabari (d. 923) with a similar content. The third great historian al-Masudi (d. 956 in Egypt) published his book on the same subject under the poetic title "Muruj al-Dhahab". These writings are not just lists of events, but contain collections of all the traditions (Hadith) about one incident, one town or one person and the authors enhanced their works with verses from the great poets of the Arab language.

When the decline of the Abbasid caliphate manifested itself and later when the Mongols ravished the Islamic countries, the centre of the Arabic-speaking part of the Islamic world passed to Egypt. From the end of the 9th century this part of the caliphate—independent from the government in Iraq—had been under the domination of the Fatimids (901—1171), the Ayyubids (1169—1250) and later the Mamelukes (1250—1517). These rulers were not of Egyptian nationality. Under the Mamelukes research into Egyptian history once again received fresh impetus. The majority of Mameluke historians wrote their works in honour of their masters. Al-Maqrizi (d. 1442) is one of the important writers among them. In his book "Doctrines and observations about the knowledge of districts and antiquities" (al-mawaiz wa'l-i'tibaer fi dikr al-hitat wa'l-atar) he tried to unite geography and history. A solid knowledge of the Pharaonic Kingdom had disappeared completely. While the Greeks mixed truth and fiction, such works in Arabic may be looked upon as more or less visionary compilations of the passage of history. A good example for this assumption is the book by Ibrahim ibn Wasif Sah al-Misri (d. before 1209) on the history of Egypt from the earliest periods until the year of his death. Since this book was finished by al-Maqrizi, it is easy to imagine the documentary value of such a compilation. Towards the end of the Mameluke period the learned scribe al-Suyuti (d. 1505) wrote a comprehensive book on the history of the caliphate in which he stressed the protector role played by the Mamelukes towards the Abbasid caliphs who had been driven out of Iraq. He called his book "Sources of purity in the stories of Imans and Caliphs". Besides these historians of a local character it is above all Ibn Khaldun (d. 1406) who gained significance. The introduction (al-Maqaddimah) to his world history is a jewel among Islamic historical writings of this time, although the remainder of the book is not up to the same standard.

Three great figures illuminate Islamic scholasticism: the Arab al-Kindi, the Turk al-Farabi and the Persian Ibn Sina. As in Christian scholasticism, philosophical and theological thought can hardly be separated. Islamic thinkers tried to prove the unity of Greek philosophy and Islamic theology. They opposed dogmatic obduracy with freedom of thought. The Arab al-Kindi (2nd half of the 9th century), called the "philosopher of the Arabs", was the first to make Plato and Aristotle accessible to Islamic thinking. In his opinion the exact sciences have their roots in Neo-Pythagoreanism. The speculative remodelling of Greek philosophers received broad dimensions when a particular school of dogmatism, the Mu'tazila, used Greek philosophy to support its own theses. The Abbasid caliph al-Ma'mum (ruled from 813—833) raised the Mu'tazila to a state doctrine and persecuted all other dogmas with fire and sword. The main works of Plato, Plotinus, Aristotle, Hippocrates, Galen and the Neo-Pythagorean schools were translated into Arabic in a very short time. The family of the Christian physician Hunain ibn Ishaq (Lat. Johannitius, d. 873), who was private physician to the Caliph al-Mutawakkil, occupied an important position among the translators. Hunain had travelled widely in the known world at that time, had studied medicine in Alexandria and settled down in Iraq. His and his sons' translations, the parchment folios of which were paid for in gold, became the basis for later philosophy. The second, the Turk al-Farabi (Lat. Alfarabius, d. 950), wrote commentaries on Plato, Aristotle and other Greek philosophers. He was strongly influenced by mystical Neo-Platonic thought. Inspired by Plato's works on the state, he wrote a tractate on civil administration (Kitab siyasat almadina). The third, the Persian Ibn Sina (Lat. Avicenna, d. 1037), was not only a great philosopher but also a great physician. As a philosopher he is close to Neo-Platonism and al-Farabi. His philosophy was mainly inspired by physics, mathematics and metaphysics, whereby he understood mathematics as an abstraction of physics and metaphysics as the abstract form of mathematics. His commentaries on Aristotle, most of which were translated in Spain, attracted lively interest. His "Canon of Medicine" (al-Qanun fi'l-Tibb)—translated into Latin by Gerard of Cremona—influenced university life until the Middle Ages. Professors of the University of Louvain used this Canon as textbook until 1650.

On the Iberian peninsula—which soon became the centre of Western Islam—the Moorish philosopher and physician Ibn Rushd (Averroes, d. 1198), had a great influence on the history of scholasticism. Some thirty to forty years after his death his commentaries on the Greek philosophers were translated into Latin and had a direct influence on Thomas Aquinas (d. 1274). The Islamic as well as the Christian Orthodox Church condemned the works of Averroes soon after their publication. His handbook of medicine "Kitab al-Kulliyyat" was translated under the name "Colliget" in Padua in 1255. If all the previously mentioned philosophers sought to prove the unity of philosophy and theology, the Persian al-Razid (Lat. Rhazes, d. 925), negated this unity. His philosophy betrays traces of Gnostic thinking, in physics he was influenced by Democritus and followed a similar doctrine in his own atomic theory, and in ethics he was close to Socrates. His philosophical writings were eclipsed by his medical works. He was the first to describe smallpox and measles according to their symptoms. He wrote a number of medical treatises, one of which, "Kitab al-Mansuri"—"Liber and Almansorem"—he dedicated to his Persian master. Between Rhazes and Avicenna comes ibn al-Abbas (Lat. Haly Abbas, d. 994). His book "Al-Kitab al-Malaki" was translated in 1127 as "Liber Regius" and is the most important medical book before Avicenna's "Canon". Ibn Abi Umsaibi'a (d. 1270), a physician, who worked for a short time in Cairo, informs us about the living conditions of physicians.

The Islamic astronomers and mathematicians are also of great significance. Under the reign of the Abbasid Caliph al-Mutawakkil, the astronomer al-Farghani (lat. Alfarganus) erected a water level gauge on the territory of the present capital Cairo. His "Introduction to the science of the phenomenon of stars" (al-Mudhil ail 'ilm hayat al-Afiek) was translated into Latin by Johan of Seville in 1135. Abu Mashar (d. 886) from Balh worked more in the field of astrology, and in the Christian Middle Ages he was considered an authority in this field. But his astrological writings aside, he was also a serious research worker. Here—as in the scholastic field—the two things are not easily separated. His Kitab al-Mudhal al-Kabir was translated by Johan Hispalensis into Latin with the title "Introductorium in astronomiem. Albumasaris Abalachii". The most important astronomer, Ali ibn Yunus, (d. 1009) lived at the court of the Fatimid Caliph al-Hakim. Already in Islam's golden age, Islamic Persians worked mainly in this field. When the Fatimids conquered Egypt they established astronomy there as well. Caliph al-Hakim had an observatory established in the neighbourhood of Cairo to promote these studies. Ibn Yunus worked there and as the result of long years of observation, he published the "Great Hakimite Star Chart" (az-Zig al-Kabir al-Hakimi) which was a revised edition of the older Persian chart. He discovered the prosthaspheric formula in spheric trigonometry. The second important scholar in this field, the physician and mathematician Ibn al-Haytham (Lat. Alhazam, d. 1038), also lived at the time of Caliph al-Hakim. But he was persecuted because he could not regulate the inundations of the Nile as he had boasted. Until the death of the caliph he feigned madness and worked in secret on his scientific research. He was rehabilitated after al-Hakim's death in 1020.

His greatest discoveries were in optics; his most important work exists only in the Latin translation "Opticae thesaurus Alhazeni Arabis libri septem". This book was known and used by Johannes Kepler. The great mathematician al-Khwarizmi (d. about 850) is the key figure in transmitting numerical notation to the Latin Western world. Despite the translation of the Indian "Siddhanta" in 771 in Baghdad, Indian numerals did not spread very quickly in the Islamic countries, and actually only al-Khwarizmi and his contemporary al-Hasib took up the eminent innovation. In general numerals were only fully adopted in the 11th century. Translated by Gerard of Cremona, the "Rules of Restoration and Reduction" (Kitab al jabr wa'l-muqabala) of al-Khwarizmi had a tremendous influence on Europe. His name still lives in our "algorism" as does "algebra" which is derived from the title of the above work.

Belles-Lettres

Of the many works of literature we are interested here in only two which were frequently illustrated. Towards the end of the 10th century the master of Arabic style al-Hariri (d. 1122) published his Maqamat (al-Maqamat) which with regard to form and content illustrates the structure of Arabic prose. Fifty tales, each complete in itself, make up this work which is written in an ornate rhymed prose excellently suited to Arabic with its many similar sounding words. The tales are told by the rascal Abu Zayd—who engages the sympathies of the reader—and the anecdotes by the traveller Harit ibn-Hammam. It is to the Persian al-Isfahani (d. 966) that we owe the largest collection of ancient Arabic poetry which he collected in his "Book of Songs" (Kitab al-Agani). It contains not only the verses of poets but also information about their living conditions. This work consisted of 20 volumes.

Libraries

The rarities already mentioned, just as those that follow, were to be found in the large libraries. Rich Muslims either collected privately precious codices and treatises on special subjects or they gave money for the building of a mosque to which a library was attached. This latter form was often chosen by the potentates of the Islamic world. Documents for such gifts by the Circassian Mameluke sultans who ruled over Egypt from 1382—1515 are still in existence. Thirdly, libraries were sometimes used as a kind of academy. One of the most famous is the "House of Wisdom" which the Abbasid Caliph al-Ma'mun founded as a meeting place for the Mu'tazila. The followers of this sect based their ideas on those of Greek, Indian and Persian philosophers whose works were available in the original and also in translations in this library, which also had an observatory attached to it. Here the most famous mathematicians and astronomers of the era met. In 1005 this institute served as a model for the foundation of a similar "House of Wisdom" in Cairo under the patronage of the Caliph al-Hakim. It was a complete replica, including the observatory. The library was open to all who wanted to read or to copy. Most scholars and translators received paper, ink and reed pen free of charge and it was quite normal to receive free board and lodging as well. The fame of princes and other Muslims was much enhanced by sponsoring scholars and artists. The Cairo library was destroyed in the 11th century. The historian al-Maqrizi tells us that in 1068 a rebel vizier ordered twenty-five camel-loads of books to be carried away. But it was not only such dangerous "book-lovers" who destroyed these places of learning; there were also the religious fanatics who tore up books, made sandals from the leather bindings and cast the written papyrus sheets to the flames or on to a heap near the pillaged palace to be burnt later. During the 15th century al-Maqrizi himself saw such heaps of books near the destroyed Fatimid palaces.

The new Turkish rulers of Egypt were no enemies of education, indeed they promoted still another form of educational institution attaching colleges to mosques. Spiritual father of these schools was the Iraqi vizier Nizam al-Mulk who founded one of the most famous of these colleges, the Nizamiya, in 1067. These colleges also provided free board and lodging to students from other parts of the country. Famous scholars taught law, theology, grammar, and philosophy in the broadest sense of the words at these colleges. Early in the Fatimid period the Caliph Al-Azis (ruled from 975—996) added a college to the newly-built Azhar Mosque in Cairo. The Azhar developed into one of the most important centres of Islamic education, a position it still maintains today. The Circassian Mamelukes also favoured this form. The Fatimid al-Azis charged his vizier Ya'qub ibn Killis to install a library in his palace. This library is later said to have possessed numerous calligraphic masterpieces: a number of copies of the famous Annalea by Al-Tabar; many important natural science works as well as Arabic dictionaries, which could be compared with our encyclopaedias. It is said that the library occupied forty rooms in the palace.

All libraries, including the private ones, were open to every scholar. Like the above mentioned Fatimid library many of them suffered a sad fate. The Islamic treasures not only fell victim to religious animosity, but also to huge fires. In 1237 the library of the Mosque of the Prophet in Medina was burnt down due to carelessness. Wars, too, took their toll of the libraries. Crusaders set fire to the huge collection at Tripolis which contained 3,000,000 volumes. The most important libraries of the Abbasid era were destroyed during the Mongol invasion. It is, nevertheless, surprising how many of these works have been preserved and are now to be found in both Oriental and Western libraries.

Illuminated Manuscripts

Miniatures are the most charming embellishments of Islamic book art. Generally Islam is said to have prohibited pictures, but to judge by the preserved monuments, this could not have been taken too seriously. The Koran contains no direct prohibition. The sources of our knowledge for this rejection are the works of the Tradition from the 9th century on the one hand, the law collection of the four big law schools on the other. Texts from Mohammed's life-time tell us that the walls of private homes and religious buildings were decorated with pictures in pre-Islamic Arabia. Muslims distinguished between the depiction of living beings and inanimate objects. According to the tradition of Buhari, Libas 94, the Archangel Gabriel did not enter the house of the Prophet, and when Mohammed complained, Gabriel said to him: "We do not enter a house in which there is a picture or a dog." The point of departure for the Islamic prohibition is probably the word "created by God" and "to illustrate" which are the same in Arabic. Behind this idea is a religious philosophy according to which illustrations can

be animated by a certain ritual—as testified to by similar ideas from the whole of the ancient Near East. Thus the artist presumes to have a certain power which belongs to Allah alone, but he cannot—like Allah—create and give life to his pictures. Pure decoration is not acknowledged in this theology, because every picture—including the decorative figure—is waiting to come to life. On Judgement Day the artist will be damned for all eternity to try and infuse the breath of life into his pictures. Tattooing, usury and pictorial art are judged by the same measure.

During their wars of conquest the Muslims saw many churches richly decorated with pictures. After they had taken Ctesiphon in Iraq, the Muslims used the main church for their prayers without taking offence at the fact that its walls were covered with pictures. Later laws stipulate quite clearly that a Muslim is not allowed to pray under pictures. He should also refuse to take a meal in a house where the pictures of living creatures offend his eyes. The Arab historian Azraki (d. 858) reports in his history of Mecca that in 630 the Prophet had all pictures, with the exception of those of Mary and Jesus, destroyed in the Ka'ba, the sacred shrine of Islam. It is not possible to lay down a general rule because the Prophet did not prohibit all depictions of living creatures. The depiction of animals was permitted on cushions and carpets, objects on which one could sit and walk—presumably an act of profanation. Inanimate objects, such as plants and architecture, do not fall under this prohibition. The law permits the depiction of living beings if it is clear that they are not capable of living. The reason for these instructions is the fear that people might take them to be graven images and pray to them.

Whether or not it was the Jews or Jewish converts who caused the Muslims to take such an attitude is something to which no clear answer can be given today. It may be assumed, however, that neither the Prophet nor the Muslims bothered much about pictures as there is no mention of it in the Koran—the earliest Arab source. These traditions—in the written form—stem from the 9th century, although they are said to have existed in a similar form a century previously. But about one century nothing is known, i.e. that century in which the first Arab caliphs, the Omayyads, built magnificent hunting lodges in Syria and Palestine: it is the decorative painting in these hunting lodges that drew the attention of scholars to the prohibition of pictures. The iconoclastic controversy that broke out in the Byzantine empire during the 8th century has no parallel among the Muslims. The Patriarch of Damascus, Saint John (Johannes Damascenus), who was also comptroller to the Caliph Abd al-Malik (ruled from 705—715) took a stand in defence of the veneration of holy images but never mentions the Muslims in his utterances or writings. Seen against the arts practised at the Omayyad courts this testimony assumes special importance. The Abbasid Caliphs who succeeded the Omayyads also promoted art in Iraq.

Islamic art received much from Christian Byzantium and the Persian empire. Through the centuries art in Byzantium and the Persian empire evolved to a characteristic form that was adopted and modified by the Muslims. From the 9th century when the country began to develop into a state, there is much proof of pictorial art in Egypt, too. Literary sources testify that the second ruler of the brief Tulunid Dynasty, Humarawaih (ruled from 884—896), had coloured wooden statues of singing girls in his palace. During the rule of the Fatimid Caliph al-Mustansir (ruled from 1035—1054) the Vizier al-Yazuiri sponsored book illustrators and painters who, in these times, were as esteemed as the calligraphers. Eighty years later Caliph al-Amir (ruled from 1101—1110) had portraits of several poets hung in the gallery of his belvedere (Manzara). Of all this nothing has been preserved but a few

fragments which indicate the heights to which this art rose. At this time Egypt was influenced by Coptic-Byzantine and Iraqi art. The Austrian National Library has a paper fragment from the 10th century depicting a horseman riding into the attack: his posture is that of a mounted Coptic saint. This fragment introduces us to the art of illustrative drawing.

Book painting was already known to the Muslims: literary sources mention illustrated books from the 9th/10th century in Iraq produced under the influence of Manichaeans whose books were publicly burnt in 923 after the prohibition of the Manichaean faith. The next example from the 11th century shows two men bearing spears and separated by an ornamental tree. Above this picture the illustrator set a line of Kufic script in white on a black ground. The floral scrolls on the letters indicate the decadence of the Kufic which, since then, has been used for decoration only. Compared with the rider these two figures have that stiffness which is characteristic of later Mameluke book paintings. As on the paper fragment the head on a fragment of mural, said to originate from a Fatimid bath of the 11th century, carries a halo. The young drinker is sitting under a round arch lifting a glass of wine to his

Horseman attacking, pen drawing, Vienna

lips. Although the painter gave more life to this picture, the U-form of the face corresponds to that of the spear *113* carriers on the paper fragment. The ivory piece also dates to the 11th century. At the top is a mounted falconer, in the centre a man bearing weapons is off to war, and at the bottom a nobleman in a palanquin is riding a camel. There is no line separating the pictures and the background has an interlaced ornament.

A few observations will precede the examples of Islamic book illumination. Of book illumination prior to the 13th century hardly anything has been preserved: the events of the 13th century destroyed most of the libraries and the conquerors suppressed the art-loving dynasties for which most artists at that time worked. Until the 13th century illumination was centred on Iraq. It was only after the Mongol invasion which concluded with the conquest of Baghdad in 1258 that the artists emigrated to states like Iraq, which were beginning to gain in influence and where the Mongols adapted themselves quickly to Islam, and to the Mameluke kingdoms of Syria and Egypt, where Eastern invasion was finally stopped near Ayn Jalut in 1260. Thus, the clear delineation of the individual schools was lost and it is extremely difficult to determine the origin of the respective manuscripts. Another difficulty for us lies in the fact that the illuminators copied older works, so that the period of origin of the miniatures remains obscure. Criteria are the date of the manuscript and the name of the copyist. Islamic book illumination begins with translations of scientific works from the Greek and Persian.

The illustrator copied the original exactly, as can—in some cases—be proven. From Arabic literature the artists would appear to have chosen two works: the Maqamat by Hariri and the Book of Songs by Isfahani.

Islamic book illumination contains Persian, Byzantine and Chinese traditions. The latter were imported by Mongols. A central perspective in the European sense is quite unknown to miniatures. Far Eastern influences of categorized perspectives as well as delicate colours are, in the main, limited to Iran. In Egypt, too, faces showed strong Mongol features. Our examples are not all from Egypt, but they were chosen with the object of giving the reader a more comprehensive impression of this art. From the golden age of Iraqi book illumination comes a page *114* from a book on horse ailments and their treatment by Ibn Al-Ahnaf. This miniature is the introduction to a chapter. The painter dispensed with all spatial detail and the grass is indicated with green stripes and stylized herbs. The colour is evenly applied between the fine contours. The double page with an anatomic painting of the eyeball *115* stems from a manuscript about eye diseases by the famous physician and translator Hunain ibn Ishaq. This manuscript may have been written at the beginning of the 13th century in Egypt. The prominent artist al-Badri illuminated 20 volumes of the "Book of Songs" under the sponsorship of Sultan Badr ad-Din Lu'lu who resided in Mosul from 1218 to 1259. On the title pages of 6 volumes he depicted throned rulers in dispute. Soon after the completion of the work the depictions were identified as

116 those of the sponsor. Our example shows the sultan amidst his princely court. The style took stiff ornamental forms to express the dignity and the inaccessibility of the ruler.

126 Similar remarks can be made about the second example. The "Book of Antitoxins" comes from the scientific sphere and is said to have been written in Mosul during the first half of the 13th century. The scene is set in an

126 apple orchard. To the left are the dolls into which the snakes inject their poison. To the right a physician with tongs is speaking to the adepts behind him. All living beings—with the exception of the snakes—have haloes—a custom which the Muslims took from Byzantine iconography. We will finish our survey of Iraqi book illumination with three pages from a manuscript about animals compiled from works by Aristotle and Ibn-Bahtisu. The manuscript was written before the Mongol invasion and shows Persian characteristics. Due to the excellent illumination work and through comparison with others from the same period and place researchers have localized it as

125 coming from Baghdad. The first page possibly shows the Persian Ibn-Bahtisu talking to the seated Aristotle. Both are painted with a halo and both have the beard of a sheikh—which was obligatory when depicting such authorities. The ornamentation of the coat of the standing person gives no indication of depth, and the folds in the coat of the seated man are likewise indicated with orna-

125 mented lines. The second sheet shows a carrion-vulture: this picture is striking because of the very bold lines of the inner plumage and the renunciation of a natural illustration in favour of a simplification close to that of a vignette. Without text it would be difficult to identify.

125 This is also true of the third page which contains a new element, the stylized tree, from which a bustard, disturbed by a bird of prey, is flying. Here, too, the bold lines of the plumage are striking. The manuscript of an astrological article by Abu Ma'sar was probably published in Cairo at about the same time—1250. The book was illustrated by a Persian illuminator in Egypt. The page shows Mercury

127 and Jupiter Sagittarius in the centre and the five planets below. These "planets" (from left to right) are Mars, the Sun, the important Saturn, the Moon and Venus. They had a great influence on human beings, formed their characters and determined their fates. It is interesting for us that a Persian was able to continue his art in this manner at a Mameluke sultan's court, since all following examples are quite different.

After the Syrian-Egyptian Mameluke Kingdom had come into being, the new Mongol-Chinese tendencies were suppressed and the artists were obliged to cultivate

Page from a book about chivalry:
Men with staves, Cairo

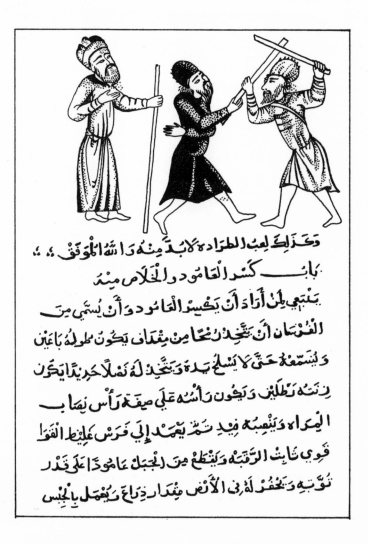

101 Tax order, with clay seal, papyrus, Cairo

102 Protocol with Islamic faith formula in stamp script, Cairo
   Tax pass, clear cursive script without diacritical points, Cairo

103 Inside book cover, Berlin

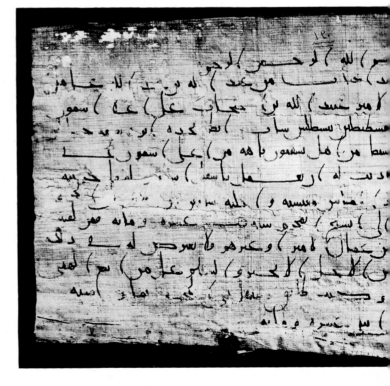

102

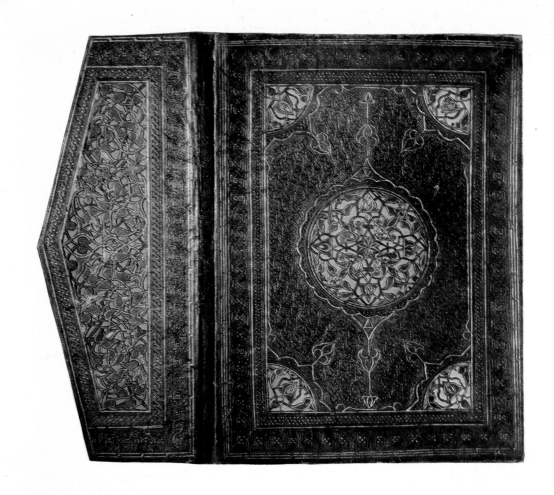

104 Book cover, Cairo
     Inside book cover, Berlin

105 Recto of same cover, Berlin

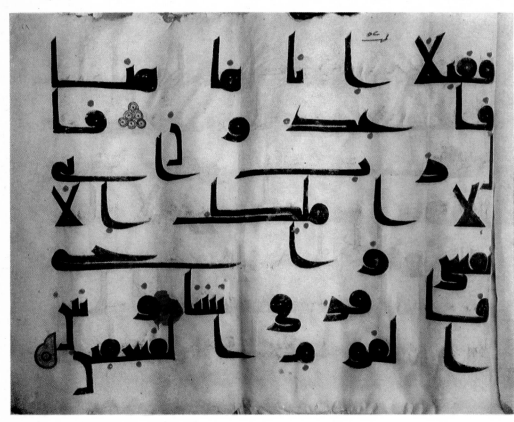

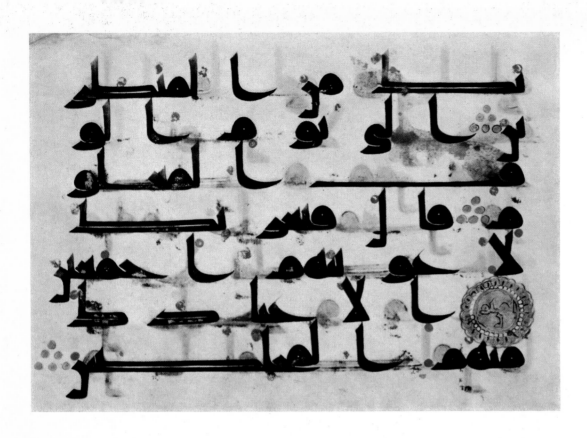

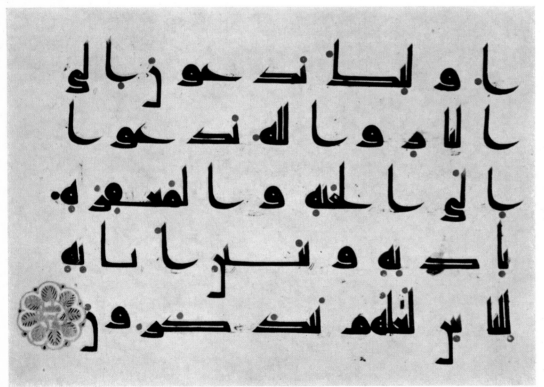

108 Page from a Koran manuscript, Kufic script, Washington
Page from a Koran manuscript, Kufic script, Washington

109 Page from a Koran manuscript, Naskhi script, Dublin

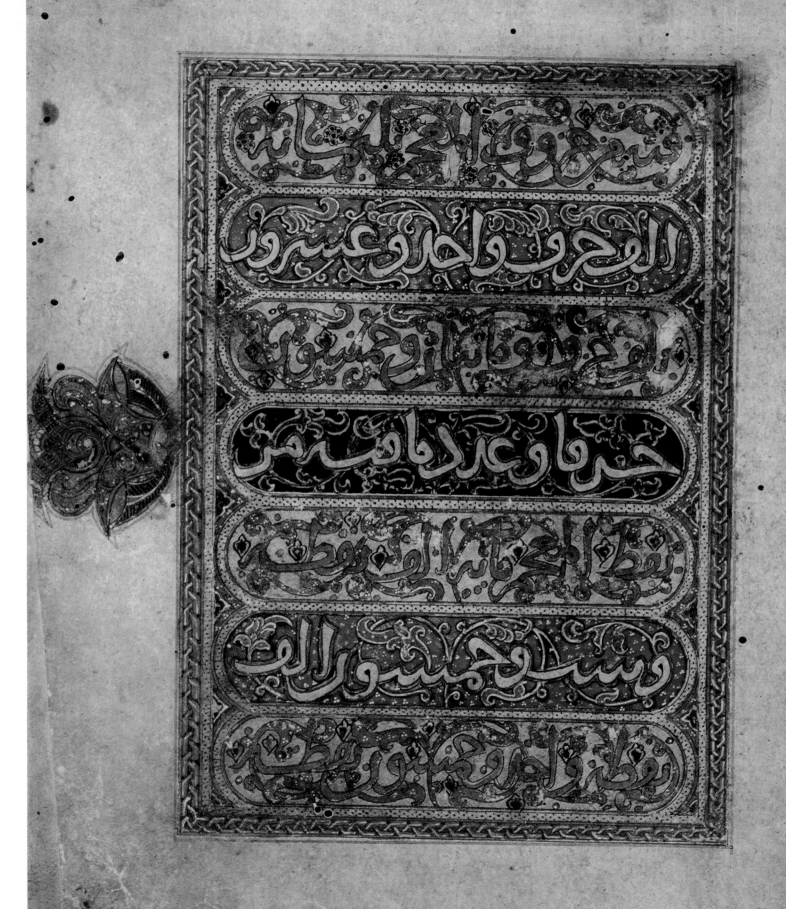

 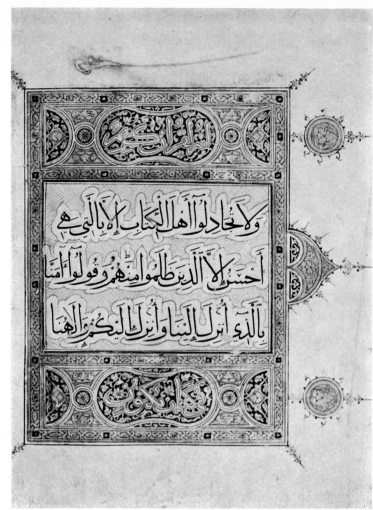

Double title picture from a Koran manuscript, Washington
Page from a Koran manuscript, Washington

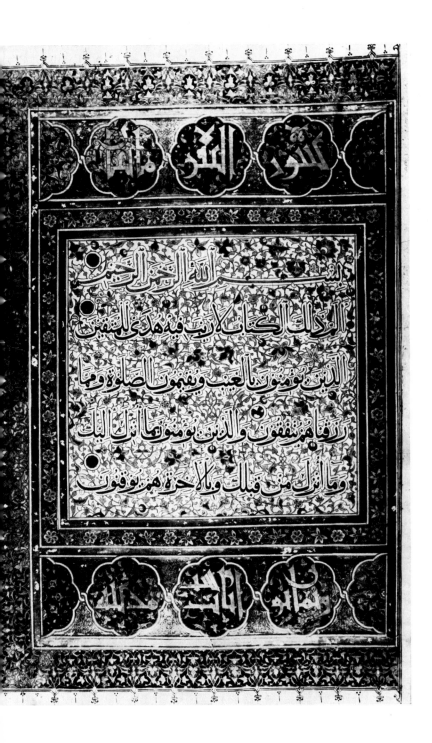

Ornamental border with falconer, spear carrier and camel with palanquin, Cairo
Man drinking, fresco from a bath, Cairo

عيينو ومن الشافنج خزمين ومن أصل الخار دج
والكزبرة البرية من كل واحد عشرة أصلا ومن الدواء المسمى
كرو بأدر ومن عنب الثعلب عشر اصول خلط جميعا ويطبخ
حتى يبقى قدر رطل ثم يعصر ويصفى ويوجر به الدابة وهذه صورته
المحموم

الباب الرابع والعشرون
في الحكة والجرب والبرص وغيره

Page from a book about horse ailments and their treatment, Cairo

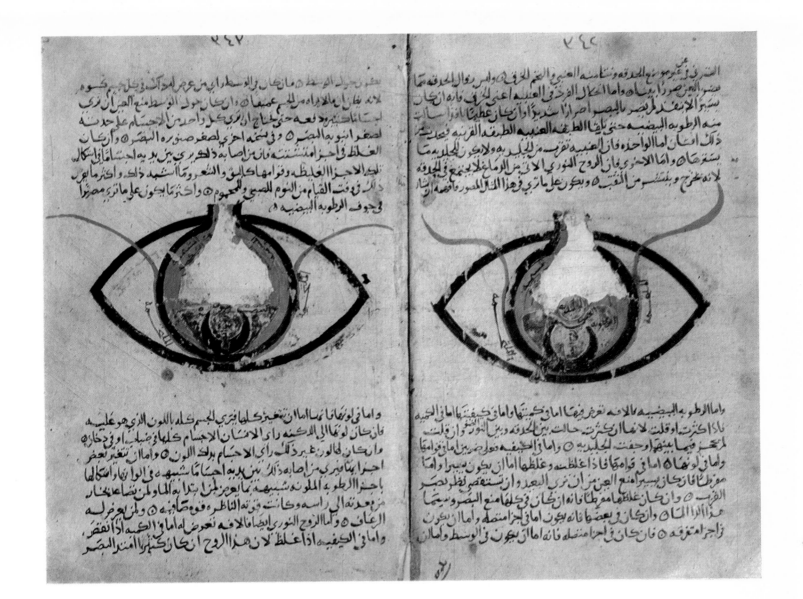

Two pages from a treatise on the eye, miniature, Cairo

Title miniature from the "Book of Songs", Cairo

Miniature from the "Book of Songs", Cairo

Garden scene miniature from the Maqamat of al-Hariri, Vienna

118

Drinking scene miniature from the Maqamat of al-Hariri, Vienna

Scene in a room, miniature from the Maqamat of al-Hariri,
London
Scene in a tent, miniature from the Maqamat of al-Hariri,
London

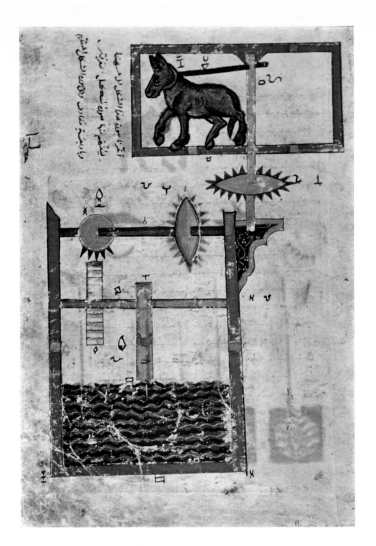

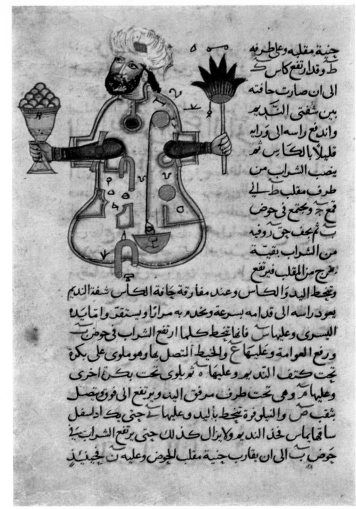

Water pump, miniature from the Automata of al-Gazari, New York

Device for drinking parties, miniature from the Automata of al-Gazari, New York

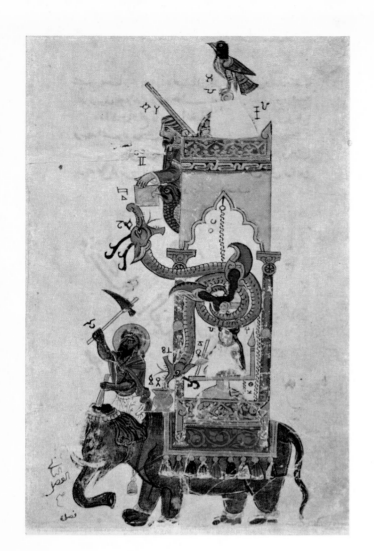

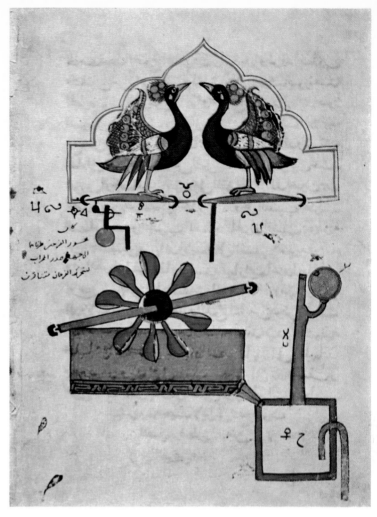

Elephant clock, miniature from the Automata of al-Gazari,
New York
Peacock water-clock, miniature from the Automata of
al-Gazari, New York

Vessel for pouring wine, miniature from the Automata of
al-Gazari, New York
Water clock in the form of a mounted man, miniature from
the Automata of al-Gazari, New York

فصعد فجعل يتأمل عينيه ويسأله عن خبره فقص عليه خبره

مع الدب وسأله أن يفتح له باب المكيدة في الخلاص من يده فقال
له القرد للخبيث أني ساحمله على السحر فلحيل لنفسك فانتهاز

124 Bear and two monkeys, miniature from a book of
fables by Bidpai, Washington

125 Aristotle and Ibn-Bahtisu disputing, miniature from
a book about animals, London
Bustard disturbed by bird of prey, miniature from
a book about animals, London
Carrion vulture, miniature from a book about
animals, London

الحكيم المولود بهذا الطالع تكون دري اللون يعلو بياض قهو نهاري مص حار يابس طبيعته من صفراو

Page from a book on chivalry:
Two men testing weapons, Cairo
Page from a book on chivalry:
Two horsemen jousting, Cairo

the old Turkish elements. The constructor and engineer al-Gazari—who lived at the court of Sultan al-Malik-al Salih (ruled from 1200—1222) in Amid (Northern Iraq)—built a number of amusing instruments for the Sultan. It was under his orders that the engineer put down his knowledge in a book on "Knowledge and Working Methods for Constructions" which was copied again in Syria in 1315. The book can be divided into the following chapters: a) construction of clocks, b) building of water vehicles, c) manufacture of goblets and jugs, d) construction of water pumping machines. The engineer used the teachings of Archimedes and Apollonius and added construction drawings of which we show six miniatures from *121,122* three chapters (a, c, d).
123

The Maqamat by Hariri is probably one of the most illuminated of Arab manuscripts. The manuscript of the British Museum comes from Syria and is dated about 1300. On both pages the viewer looks into an interior, one an open tent and the other a richly furnished chamber. *120* The disputing parties all have haloes. The clothing is decorated in such a fashion that folds recede. In the manuscript of the National Library in Vienna, which was written 30 years later, the figures are depicted on a *118* framed golden background. Here, too, the ornamentation

of dress is striking. The whole has the effect of a stage, *119* particularly when the feet and hands of the figure project into the margin. The only comparison is the Turkish shadow play with its figures of coloured leather which were moved behind a white parchment skin. This pattern was followed for the scene in the garden as well as for the drinking party. The golden background was also used for miniatures in which nature was depicted. The example shown here comes from the wide realm of Indo-Persian animal fables, the illustrations to which were extremely popular among the Muslims. A bear is talking to two *124* monkeys who are sitting on the branches of a tree listening to him. This illumination is of a slightly more recent date than the Maqamat miniatures. Animal depictions were far more lively than those of people, probably because less convention had to be observed.

A retrograde step is shown in the figures from a manuscript about chivalry from the 14th century. The frame has vanished and the pictures are mere explanatory illustrations of the text. The heterogeneous character of the Mameluke rulers in Egypt is quite clearly revealed. They are exercising themselves in the stave game, caring for their weapons, keeping their bows flexible at the gallows or jousting with other knights. *128*

Captions to the Illustrations

89 *Burial stele of Ibn Hair*. The stele was erected 12 years after the conquest of Egypt. The inscription is an example of the angular script from which Kufic developed. Museum of Islamic Art, Cairo. Limestone. Fustat, 652.

98 *Horseman attacking*. National Library Vienna, PERF No. 954. Pen drawing on paper, Size: 8×10.4 cms. Egypt; 10th century, Published by J. Karabacek in: Mitteilungen aus der Sammlung der Papyri Erzherzog Rainer V, 1892, page 123 and following

99 *Two men carrying spears*. Over them a line in Kufic script. Museum of Islamic Art, Cairo, Cat. No. 13703. Indian ink on paper. Egypt; 11th century

100 *Men with staves*. Page from a book about chivalry. Museum of Islamic Art, Cairo, Cat. No. 18019. Paper, Egypt; 15th century

101 *Tax order of Qurra ibn Sarik, governor of Egypt, to the community of Psiru in central Egypt*. Above: simple cursive script with several diacritical points; below: Greek translation of the text. Originally rolled, at foot clay seal. National Library Cairo, Cat. No. 335. Papyrus. Egypt; written 709/10.

Published by A. Grohmann, Arabic Papyri in the Egyptian Library, III, Document 160, Cairo 1938

102 *Protocol with Islamic faith formula in stamp script*. The line of Arabic text has two lines of Greek translation above it. Both hands are extremely difficult to decipher. National Library Cairo, Catalogue No. 6, Stamp script on papyrus. Egypt, early 8th century. Published by A. Grohmann, Arabic Papyri in the Egyptian Library I, Document 1, Cairo 1934

102 *Tax pass*. A clear cursive script without diacritical points; at the end of the roll a clay seal with name of the scribe. A man from Upper-Ashmumain is thus authorized to work in Lower-Ashmumain and to pay taxes there. National Library Cairo, Cat. No. 130. Papyrus. Ashmumain, dated 731. Published by A. Grohmann, Arabic Papyri in the Egyptian Library III, Document 175, Cairo 1938

103 *Inside book cover*. Staatliche Museen zu Berlin, Islamische Abteilung, Cat. No. I. 857. Leather, punched and painted. 50×39 cms. Egypt; 14th/15th century

104 *Book cover*. National Library Cairo, Ar. g/48, Ar 9/38. Leather, punched and painted. Egypt; 14th century

104 *Inside book cover*. Staatliche Museen zu Berlin, Islamische Abteilung, Cat. No. I. 877. Leather, punched and painted, 53.5×39.5 cms. Egypt; 14th/15th century

105 *Recto of same cover*

106 *Page from a Koran manuscript*. Kufic of an ancient character without diacritical points. National Library Cairo, Ma Sahif 139. Parchment. 7th century

106 *Page from a Koran manuscript*. Kufic with diacritical points. National Library Cairo. Parchment. 9th century

107 *Page from a Koran manuscript*. Kufic with calligraphically styled diacritical points. An ornamented line separates the suras. In the lower left-hand corner the ink has corroded the parchment. National Library Cairo, Ma Sahif 1, 8th century. Next to it: Note about the alleged scribe Imam Ja'far with diacritical points and signs for vowels in normal book writing. Paper, Middle Ages

108 *Page from a Koran manuscript*. Kufic script with diacritical points in red; the script on the verso can be faintly seen. Freer Gallery of Art, Washington, 30.66 R. Parchment. 9th century

108 *Page from a Koran manuscript*. Kufic in the beautiful, elegant form of the late period. Freer Gallery of Art, Washington, 37.6 V. Parchment. Egypt, 10th century

109 *Page from a Koran manuscript*. Naskhi script, written by Ibn al-Bawwab. Chester Beatty Library, Dublin, No. 1431. Parchment. 10th century. Published by D. S. Rice, The Unique Ibn al-Bawwab Manuscript in the Chester Beatty Library, Dublin 1955

110 *Double title picture from a Koran manuscript*. Two lines of near-Kufic in white stand on the page which is decorated with coloured arabesques. Such manuscripts were often made for the Mameluke sultans. Freer Gallery of Art, Washington, 30.55. Paper. Egypt. 14th century

110 *Page from a Koran manuscript*. Naskhi script (Thulut). The script is framed by a golden arabesque. The letters are set off from the gilded network. The diacritical points and vowel signs are clearly distinguishable. Freer Gallery of Art, Washington, 32.60. Paper. 14th century

111 *Page from a Koran manuscript*. Naskhi script, written by al-Musta'simi; an example of "classic Naskhi". National Library Cairo, Cat. No. 8493. Paper, Iraq; 1290

111 *Page from a Koran manuscript for the Sultan Mu'ayyad*. Naskhi script (Rihani), above and below Kufic script. National Library Cairo, Cat. No. 9999. Paper. Egypt, between 1412 and 1421

112 *Page of the manuscript "The Tradition" by al-Shafi'i*. Naskhi script with diacritical points and comments in different hands. National Library Cairo, Cat. No. 33856. Paper. Egypt, about 1160

112 *Page of the manuscript "Collection of the Tradition"*. By Abd Allah ibn Wahb, Naskhi script with diacritical points. Only preserved Arabic papyrus codex. National Library Cairo, Hadith 32/2. Papyrus. Egypt. End of the 9th century. Published by I. Weil, in: Mémoires de l'Institut Français d'Archéologie Orientale au Caire 68, 1935, 177 and following

113 *Ornamental border with falconer, spear carrier and camel with palanquin*. Museum of Islamic Art, Cairo, Cat. No. 5024. Ivory. Egypt. 11th century

113 *Man drinking*. Fresco from a Fatimid bath. Museum of Islamic Art, Cairo, Cat. No. 12880, Egypt, 11th century

114 *Page from a book about horse ailments and their treatment*. Above the chapter heading, a vignette depicting a man and horse. National Library Cairo, No 8 f, alil Aga. Paper. Baghdad; written in 1209

115 *Miniature on two pages from a treatise on the eye*. Translated and compiled from Galen and Hippocrates by Hunain ibn Ishaq. National Library Cairo, 100 Tibb Taimur. Paper. Egypt, 13th century

116 *Title miniature from the "Book of Songs"*. Throned ruler surrounded by court officials and musicians. The miniature is the work of al-Badri. The Mongolian influence is marked. National Library Cairo, Adab 579. Paper, 31×22 cms. Iraq; 1208/09. Published by A. Monsa, Zur Geschichte der islamischen Buchmalerei in Ägypten, Cairo, 1931, page 38, illustration 16

117 *Miniature from the "Book of Songs"*. Court followers in conversation. Panelled with ornamental division. National Library Cairo, Adab 579. Paper. 31×22 cms. Iraq; 1208/1209

118 *Garden scene miniature* from the Maqamat of al-Hariri. Nationalbibliothek, Vienna, AFG. Paper. Probably Egypt; 1334. Published by K. Holter in Jahrbuch der Kunsthistorischen Sammlungen in Vienna, Special No. 104, NF XI, 1937

119 *Drinking scene miniature* from the Maqamat of al-Hariri. Nationalbibliothek, Vienna, AFG. Paper. Probably Egypt; 1334. Published by K. Holter in Jahrbuch der Kunsthistorischen Sammlungen in Vienna, Special No. 104, NF XI, 1937

120 *Scene in a room*. Miniature from the Maqamat of al-Hariri. British Museum, London, Add 22114 f. 79 v. Paper. Syria; 1300. Published by W. Bruchthal, Three Illustrated Hariri Manuscripts in the British Museum, in: The Burlington Magazine 77, 1940, 144 and following

120 *Scene in a tent*. Miniature from the Maqamat of al-Hariri. British Museum, London 22114 f. 96 r. Paper. Syria; 1300. Published by W. Bruchthal, Three Illustrated Hariri Manuscripts in the British Museum, in: The Burlington Magazine 77, 1940, 144 and following

121 *Water pump*. Miniature from the Automata of al-Gazari. Metropolitan Museum of Art, New York, 55. 121.11. Paper, 31×21.9 cms. Egypt, 1315

121 *Device for drinking parties*. Miniature from the Automata of al-Gazari. Metropolitan Museum of Art, New York, 55.121.12. Paper, 31×21.9 cms. Egypt, 1315

122 *Elephant clock*. Miniature from the Automata of al-Gazari. Metropolitan Museum of Art, New York, 57.51.23. Paper, 31×21.9 cms. Egypt; 1315. Published by Ettinghausen, Arabische Malerei, Geneva, Skira, 1962, page 93

122 *Peacock water-clock*. Miniature from the Automata of al-Gazari. Metropolitan Museum of Art, New York, 55.121.15. Paper, 31×21.9 cms. Egypt; 1315

123 *Vessel for pouring wine*. Miniature from the Automata of al-Gazari. Metropolitan Museum of Art, New York, 55.121. 14. Paper, 31×21.9 cms. Egypt, 1315

123 *Water clock in the form of a mounted man*. Miniature from the Automata of al-Gazari. Metropolitan Museum of Art, New York, 55.121.13. Paper, 31×21.9 cms. Egypt; 1315

124 *Bear and two monkeys*. Miniature from a book of fables by Bidpai. Freer Gallery of Art, Washington, 54.2. Paper, 24.9×17.6 cms. Egypt; about 1335. Published by Ettinghausen, Arabische Malerei, Geneva, Skira, 1962, page 141

125 *Aristotle and Ibn-Bahtisu disputing*. Miniature from a book about animals, compiled from Aristotle and Ibn-Bahtisu. British Museum, London, Or. 2784, f 101 v. Paper. Baghdad; before 1258

125 *Bustard disturbed by bird of prey*. Miniature from a book about animals, compiled from Aristotle and Ibn-Bahtisu. British Museum, London, Or. 2784, f 228 v. Paper. Baghdad; before 1258

125 *Carrion vulture*. Miniature from a book about animals, compiled from Aristotle and Ibn-Bahtisu. British Museum, London, Or. 2784, f. 35 v. Paper. Baghdad; before 1258

126 *Miniature from the "Book of antitoxins" of the Pseudo-Galenos*. Snakes giving up poison by biting dolls. National Library, Vienna, AF 10 fol. 25 v. Paper. Mosul; early 13th century. Published by Grohmann/Arnold, Denkmäler islamischer Buchkunst, Munich 1929, Illustration 34 above

127 *Miniature from the astrological manuscript by Abu Ma'sar*. Mercury and Jupiter; below, the five planets Mars, the Sun, Saturn, the Moon and Venus. National Library, Paris. Paper. Cairo; about 1250. Published by E. Blochet, Muselman Painting XII—XVII Century, London, 1929, illustration XXXIII

128 *Two men testing weapons*. Page from a book on chivalry. Museum of Islamic Art, Cairo, Cat. No. 18235, Paper. Egypt; 15th century

128 *Two horsemen jousting*. Page from a book about chivalry. Museum of Islamic Art, Cairo, Cat. No. 18236. Paper. Egypt; 15th century

Bibliography

Abbreviation of periodicals

Äg Fo   Ägyptologische Forschungen (Egyptological research), Glückstadt-Hamburg, New York

AMAW   Abhandlungen der Mainzer Akademie der Wissenschaften, Wiesbaden (Articles of the Mainz Academy of Sciences)

APAW   Abhandlungen der Preussischen Akademie der Wissenschaften, Berlin (Articles of the Prussian Academy of Sciences)

APF   Archiv für Papyrusforschung und verwandte Gebiete, Leipzig

BGU   Ägyptische Urkunden aus den Staatlichen Museen zu Berlin, Griechische Urkunden, Berlin

BKT   Berliner Klassikertexte, Berlin

JEA   The Journal of Egyptian Archaeology, London

MDAIK   Mitteilungen des Deutschen Archäologischen Instituts, Abt. Kairo, Wiesbaden (Articles of the German Institute of Archaeology, Department Cairo)

UGAAe   Untersuchungen zur Geschichte und Altertumskunde Aegyptens, Leipzig (Investigations in the History and Archaeology of Egypt)

ZÄS   Zeitschrift für Ägyptische Sprache und Altertumskunde, Berlin and Leipzig (Review of Egyptian Language and Archaeology)

The Pharaonic Period

BARGUET, P., *Le Livre des Morts des anciens Égyptiens*, Paris 1967

BISSING, W., FREIHERR VON, *Die Verwendung von Musterbüchern im Alten Reich*, ZÄS 53, 1917, page 148 and following

BRUNNER, H., *Altägyptische Erziehung*, Wiesbaden 1957

BRUNNER, H., *Die Lehre des Cheti, Sohnes des Duauf* Äg Fo 13, 1944

BRUNNER-TRAUT, *Die Altägyptischen Scherbenbilder (Bildostraka) der deutschen Museen und Sammlungen*, Wiesbaden 1956

BRUNNER-TRAUT, *Die Weisheitslehre des Djedef-Hor*, ZÄS 76, 1940, page 3 and following

ČERNÝ, J., *Paper and Books in Ancient Egypt*, London 1952

DERCHAIN, P., *Le Papyrus Salt 825 (B.M. 10051), rituel pour la conservation de la vie en Égypte*, Academie Royale de Belgique Mémoires 58, Brussels 1965

ERMAN A., *Die Literatur der Aegypter*, Leipzig 1923

ERMAN, A., *Die ägyptischen Schülerhandschriften*, APAW No. 2, Berlin 1925

ERMAN, A.,—H. O. LANGE, *Papyrus Lansing*. Eine ägyptische Schulhandschrift der 20. Dynastie, Det Kgl. Danske Videnskabernes Selskab, Meddelelser X, 3, Copenhagen 1925

FECHT, G., *Die Wiedergewinnung der altägyptischen Verskunst*, MDAIK 19, 1963, page 56 and following

GARDINER, A. H., *Die Erzählung des Sinuhe und die Hirtengeschichte*. Literarische Texte des Mittleren Reiches II, Leipzig 1909

GARDINER, A. H., *Egyptian Hieratic Texts Series I: Literary Texts of the New Kingdom*, Part I: *the Pap. Anastasi I and the Pap. Koller, together with the parallel Texts*, Leipzig 1911

GARDINER, A. H., *Hieratic Papyri in the British Museum*, 3rd Series, Chester Beatty Gift, London 1935

GARDINER, A. H., *Late Egyptian Miscellanies*, Bibliotheca Aegyptiaca 7, 1937

GARDINER, A. H., *The Mansion of Life and the Master of the King's Largess*, JEA 24, 1938, page 83 and following

GARDINER, A. H., *The Instruction Addressed to Kagemni and his Brethren*, JEA 32, 1946, page 74 and following

GARDINER, A. H., *Ancient Egyptian Onomastica*, Vol. I—III, London 1947

GARDINER, A. H., *Egypt of the Pharaohs*, Oxford 1961

GLANVILLE, S. R. K., *The Legacy of Egypt*, Oxford 1942

HANDBUCH DER ORIENTALISTIK I, 1 and 2, *Ägyptische Schrift und Sprache*, Leyden 1952, 1959

HERMANN, A., *Buchillustrationen auf ägyptischen Bücherkästen*, MDAIK 15, 1957, page 112 and following

HERMANN, A., *Das Buch "Kmj.t" und die Chemie*, ZÄS 79, 1954, page 99 and following

KOROSTOVZEV, M. A., *Pisci drevnego Egipta*, Moscow 1962

LANGE, H. O., *Das Weisheitsbuch des Amenemope aus dem Papyrus 10474 des British Museum*, Det Kgl. Danske Videnskabernes Selskab, Meddelelser XI, 2, Copenhagen 1925

LANZONE, R. V., *Les Papyri du Lac Moeris*, Turin 1896

LUCAS, A., *Ancient Egyptian Materials and Industries 4th ed.* London 1963

MAYSTRE, CH.,—A. PIANKOFF, *Le Livre des Portes*, Mémoires de l'Institut Français du Caire, 74, Le Caire 1939 and following

MORENZ, S., *Ägyptische Religion*, Stuttgart 1960

MORENZ, S., *Altägyptischer Jenseitsführer Pap.* Berlin 3127, Leipzig 1964

PIANKOFF, A.,—N. RAMBOVA, *Mythological Papyri*, Bollingen Series XL, 3, New York 1957

Schott, S., *Hieroglyphen*, Untersuchungen zum Ursprung der Schrift, AMAW No. 24, 1950, page 1709 and following, Wiesbaden 1951

Sethe, K., *Die Altägyptischen Pyramidentexte*, Leipzig 1908 and following

Sethe, K., *Dramatische Texte zu altägyptischen Mysterienspielen*, UGAAe 10, 1928

Vandier d'Abbadie, J., *Catalogue des ostracas figurés de Deir el Médineh*, Documents de Fouilles de l'Institut Français d'Archéologie Orientale du Caire, Vol. 2, Le Caire 1937

Weitzmann, K., *Illustrations in Roll and Codex*, Princeton 1947

Wolf, W., *Kulturgeschichte des Alten Ägypten*, Stuttgart 1962

Žaba, Z., *Les Maximes de Ptahhotep*, Prague 1956

The Greco-Roman Period / The Coptic Book

Bell, H. I., *Egypt from Alexander the Great to the Arab Conquest*, Oxford 1948

Cramer. M., *Koptische Buchmalerei*, Recklinghausen 1964

Cramer, M., *Koptische Paläographie*, Wiesbaden 1964

Diringer, D., *The Hand-Produced Book*, London 1953

Doresse, J., *Les Livres secrets des Gnostiques d'Égypte*, I, Paris 1958

Hunger, H., *Antikes und mittelalterliches Buch- und Schriftwesen*, in: Geschichte der Textüberlieferung der antiken und mittelalterlichen Literatur, Vol. I, Zürich 1961, page 25 and following

Ibscher, H., *Bucheinbände aus Ägypten*, in: Amtliche Berichte aus den Königlichen Kunstsammlungen Berlin, 1911, page 46 and following

Ibscher, H., *Die Handschrift*, in: Manichäische Handschriften der Sammlung A. Chester Beatty, vol. 1, *Manichäische Homilien*, Stuttgart 1934, page IX and following

Ibscher, H., *Die Handschrift*, in: Manichaean Manuscripts in the Chester Beatty Collection, vol. II *A Manichaean Psalm Book*, part II, Stuttgart 1938, pages VII and following

Ibscher., H., *Die Handschrift*, in: Manichäische Handschriften der Staatlichen Museen Berlin, Vol. 1 *Kephalaia*, Stuttgart 1940, page V and following

Kapsomenos, S. G., *Der Papyrus von Dervéni*, Ein Kommentar zur orphischen Theogonie, Gnomon 35, 1963, page 222 and following

Kenyon, F. G., *Books and Readers in Ancient Greece and Rome*, 2nd edition, Oxford 1951

Krause, M., *Der Handschriftenfund bei Nag Hammadi*, Umfang und Inhalt, MDAIK Bd. 18, Wiesbaden 1962, page 121 and following

Krause, M., *Schätze aus dem zweiten großen Fund koptischer Handschriften*, in: Orientalische Literaturzeitung, LXII, 1967, No. 9/10, Sp. 437 and following

Lewis, N., *L'industrie du papyrus dans l'Égypte gréco-romaine*, Paris 1934

Metzger, B. M., *The Text of the New Testament*, Oxford 1964

Milne, H. J. M., — T. C. Skeat, *Scribes and Correctors of the Codex Sinaiticus*, 2nd edition, London 1955

Morenz, S., *Die koptische Literatur*, in: Handbuch der Orientalistik, Bd. I, Abschnitt II, Leyden 1952, page 207 and following

Morenz, S., *Das Koptische*, in: Handbuch der Orientalistik, Bd. I, Abschnitt I, Leyden 1959, page 90 and following

Pack, R. A., *The Greek and Latin Literary Texts from Greco-Roman Egypt*, 2nd edition, Ann Arbor 1965

Peremans, W., — J. Vergote, *Papyrologisch Handboek*, Leuven 1942

Preisendanz, K., *Papyrusfunde und Papyrusforschung*, Leipzig 1933

Proverbien-Kodex, Faksimile-Ausgabe, Leipzig 1963, mit Nachwort von A. Böhlig

Regemorter B. van, *Some Early Bindings from Egypt in the Chester Beatty Library*, Dublin 1958

Roberts, H. C. *The Codex*, in: Proceedings of British Academy of Science, London, XI 1954

Santifaller, L., *Beiträge zur Geschichte der Beschreibstoffe im Mittelalter*, Graz 1953

Schubart, W., *Einführung in die Papyruskunde*, Berlin 1918

Schubart, W., *Das Buch bei den Griechen und Römern*, Berlin-Leipzig, 2. Auflage, 1921, 3. Auflage (ohne Anmerkungen), Leipzig 1961

Schubart, W., *Griechische Paläographie*, München 1925 (= Handbuch der Altertumswissenschaft, 1. Bd., 4. Abt., 1. Hälfte)

Skeat, T. C., *Prehistory of the Christian Book: Papyrus and Parchment*, in: The Cambridge History of the Bible, Vol. 2, Ch. III, pages 54—79; 512 and following, Cambridge University Press 1969

Turner, E. G., *Greek Papyri*, Princeton 1968

Unnik, W. V. van, *Evangelien aus dem Nilsand*, Frankfurt a. M. 1960

The Book in Islamic Egypt

Abott, N., *The Rise of the North Arabic Script*, Chicago 1938

Arnold, Sir Thomas W., *Painting in Islam*. A Study of the Place of Pictorial Art in Muslim Culture, Oxford 1928

Becker, C. H., *Vom Werden und Wesen der islamischen Welt* (Islamstudien I), Leipzig 1924

Blochet, E., *Les illuminures des manuscrits orienteaux*, Paris 1926

El-Bokhari (al-Buḫārī), *Les Traditions islamiques*, traduits de l'arabe avec notes et index par O. Houdas et W. Marcais 4 volumes, Paris 1903—1914

BROCKELMANN, C., *Geschichte der arabischen Literatur*. 2 volumes with three supplementary volumes, 2nd ed. Vol. 1 and 2 with supplementary vols. 1—3, Leyden 1943—1949

BROCKELMANN, C., *Geschichte der islamischen Völker und Staaten*, 2nd ed. Munich/Berlin 1943

CRESWELL, A. C., *The Lawfulness of Painting in Early Islam*, In: Ars Islamica XI/XII, 1940, 159 and following

ENZYKLOPÄDIE DES ISLAMS, 1st edition, Leyden 1913—1938, 2nd edition English/French, Leyden from 1954

ETTINGHAUSEN, R., *Arabische Malerei*, Geneva 1962

FARMER, H. G., *Musik des Mittelalters: Der Islam* = Musikgeschichte in Bildern III, 2, Leipzig, no date

FÜCK, J., *Die Rolle des Traditionalismus im Islam*, in: Zeitschrift der deutschen Morgenländischen Gesellschaft 93, 1939, 1 and following

GROHMANN, A., *Einführung und Chrestomathie zur arabischen Papyruskunde*, Prague 1954

GROHMANN, A., *Arabic Papyri in the Egyptian Library*, 3 volumes, Cairo 1934—1938

GRUBE, E. J., *Miniature islamiche dal XIII al XIX secolo*, Venice 1962

AL-ḤARĪRĪ (*see* Rückert)

AL-HAWARI, H. M., *The Most Ancient Islamic Documents*, in: Journal of the Researches of Arabic Studies 1930, 321 and following

HITTI, P. K., *The History of Arabs*, 5th ed. London 1953

HUART, C., *Les Calligraphes et les Miniaturistes de l'Orient Musulman*, Paris 1908

KARABACEK, J., *Ein arabisches Reiterbild des X. Jh.*, in: Mitteilungen aus der Papyrussammlung Erzherzog Rainer V, 1892, 123 and following

DER KORAN, translated by R. Henning, explanation and comment by K. Rudolph and E. Werner, Leipzig 1968

DER KORAN, translated by R. Paret, Stuttgart 1963—1966

KÜHNEL, E., *Islamische Schriftkunst*, Berlin and Leipzig, not dated

LOREY, E. DE, *De Bestiaire de l'Escorial*, in: Gazette des Beaux Arts 77, December 1935, 228 and following

AL-MAQRĪZĪ, *al-mawāʼiz wa-ʼl-iʼtibār fi dikr al-ḥiṭaṭ wa-ʼl-ātār*, 2 volumes, Cairo-Bulāq 1853

MONSA, A., *Zur Geschichte der islamischen Buchmalerei in Ägypten*, Cairo 1931

MORITZ, B., *Arabic Palaeography*. A Collection of Arabic Texts from the first Century of the Hidjra till the Year 1000, Cairo 1905

NÖLDEKE, T., *Geschichte des Qurans*, 2 volumes, 2nd edition, Leipzig 1909 and 1919

PARET, R., *Textbelege zum Islamischen Bilderverbot*, in: Das Werk des Künstlers, FS Hubert Schrade, Stuttgart 1960, 36 and following

RÜCKERT, F., *Die Verwandlungen des Abu Seid von Serug oder die Makamen des Hariri*, Frankfurt/M. 1826

SARRE, F., *Islamische Buchkunst*, Berlin, not dated

SPULER, B., *Geschichte der islamischen Länder* I—III = Handbuch der Orientalistik VI, Leyden 1952 and following

WEIL, J., *Notice sur un manuscrit Malekite d'Abd Allah Ibn Wahb Ibn Muslim*, in: Mémoires d l'Institut Français d'Archéologie Orientale du Caire, 68, 1935, 177 and following; Arabic Text, in: Publications de l'Institut Français d'Archéologie Orientale du Caire 3, 1939

WÜSTENFELD, F., *Die Geschichte und Beschreibung der Stadt Mekka von el-Azraki*, Leipzig 1858